gardening with

# INDIGENOUS SHRUBS

DAVID & SALLY JOHNSON
GEOFF NICHOLS

First published in 2002 by Struik Publishers
(a division of New Holland Publishing (South Africa) (Pty) Ltd)
London • Cape Town • Sydney • Auckland
New Holland Publishing is a member of the Johnnic Publishing Group

Garfield House
86-88 Edgware Road
W2 2EA London
United Kingdom
www.newhollandpublishers.com

80 McKenzie Street
Cape Town
8001
South Africa
www.struik.co.za

14 Aquatic Drive
Frenchs Forest, NSW 2086
Australia

218 Lake Road
Northcote, Auckland
New Zealand

ISBN 1 86872 788 2

1 3 5 7 9 10 8 6 4 2

**Publishing manager:** Annlerie van Rooyen
**Managing editor:** Lesley Hay-Whitton
**Design director:** Janice Evans
**Designer:** Alison Day
**Editor:** Monique Whitaker
**Proofreader:** Inge du Plessis
**Indexer:** Mary Lennox



**Front cover:** *Plectranthus ecklonii*
**Back cover:** *Maytenus mossambicensis* (left), *Canavalia rosea* (middle), *Coffea racemosa* (right)
**Title page:** *Grewia flava*
**This page:** *Leonotis leonurus*

Reproduction by Hirt & Carter Cape (Pty) Ltd
Printed by Craft Print International Ltd

# CONTENTS

# INTRODUCTION

**TOP:** *Protea repens*
**MIDDLE:** *Turraea obtusifolia*
**ABOVE:** *Strophanthus speciosus*

Plant species are not evenly distributed around the globe; they are far more numerous in certain parts of the world. A fortuitous combination of climatic changes, geography and geology has favoured the evolution of new species in southern Africa. Many of these are endemic – that is, they occur only here. The south-western Cape has a very high number of endemic plants; so too does Pondoland in the Eastern Cape, and Maputaland in northeastern KwaZulu-Natal. Each of these regions has its own long list of unique flora, many of which are beautiful shrubs.

Our local plants, far from being commonplace, and of lesser status than exotics, far exceed them in interest, as we can appreciate them in their natural settings. In addition, we have so many different species of flora to enjoy, as, at the global level, South Africa happens to be a diversity hotspot.

## Gardening with indigenous shrubs

So, many of the world's most desirable garden plants grow right here in South Africa, and they are starting to gain appreciation locally. Apart from their scientific interest, there are two other compelling reasons to grow local plants. One reason is that all the animals with which they co-evolved – herbivores and pollinators, and then predators that, in turn, depend upon them – are certain to be present locally. They are more likely to take up residence in a garden that appears to them to be a natural habitat. The second reason is that the conditions in your garden will be better suited to growing indigenous plants than to growing most aliens, although the concept of a plant being indigenous to an area is often misunderstood, or misapplied.

Indigenous means homegrown, local; occurring naturally, without artificial assistance, and *in a defined place*. This last phrase is important, for everything is indigenous somewhere. South Africa, botanically speaking, is a world in one country. So defining something as 'indigenous to South Africa' is not necessarily very useful in choosing garden plants; the definition is too wide. This explains some disappointing failures, as not all indigenous plants are tough. The key to success is to concentrate upon shrubs suited to your local climate and habitat.

### *Using indigenous shrubs in the garden*

While trees make the main impact in a garden, it is shrubs that provide the backing. Many shrubs are worth growing as attractive specimens; others provide screening and variety of form. Also, there are a number of shrubs that have long flowering and fruiting seasons, filling in the 'blank spots' in the garden calendar. They are well-suited to smaller gardens, and mature more quickly than trees, so you can grow decent-sized shrubs quite quickly. Most are easily maintained, and offer extra scope for inventive planting.

Using different species provides your garden with different growth forms, which will complement each other. You can start with fast-growing, bigger shrubs, using denser species (such as *Carissa*) to take over once these first shrubs reach the leggy stage – when all the foliage is at the top of the shrub, with 'bare legs' beneath, and it no longer forms a screen.

- **Screening with shrubs** The informality created by shrubs is ideally suited to an indigenous garden, particularly where bush clumps are a feature. Bush clumps consist of a closely planted community, where two or more species are present. A bush clump sited near a boundary can be extended, in a less-than-straight line, to form a screen, without giving the appearance of doing so. If the species are correctly chosen the screen will require very little subsequent attention. Ideal screen species are densely leafy and retain foliage near ground level. *Chrysanthemoides* is a good example. The screening effect of shrubs provides more than privacy. Shrubs also reduce the effect of wind, which is especially useful at the coast and in the flatter parts of the high interior. They are more effective shelters than walls, which tend to deflect rather than halt wind. Shrubs slow wind by diffusing it.

### *Spiny shrubs*

Shrubs also provide a physical barrier, often more effective than a fence. Spiny shrubs are ideal for this purpose. Conventionally, gardeners make little use of spines, yet these have a beauty of their own, not lessened by their stark functionality. Spiny shrubs are also very useful in screens. Short, shrubby plants that retain some branches near ground level are ideal. When you plant a number of spiny shrubs close together, you can create an impenetrable barrier.

### *Scrambling shrubs*

Some shrubs use their energy quite differently from others, putting most of their resources into growing as much and as far as possible, rather than into developing a solid trunk. The result is a scrambler, unable to stand on its own. The scrambling habit, while not strictly parasitic, is definitely 'cheating', by human standards, because scramblers obtain their full share of sunshine by taking advantage of the sturdier trunks of their neighbours by literally leaning on these plants. The scramblers, therefore, save all the energy involved in growing such a trunk, while other plants have invested years of growth in producing theirs.

By economising on trunk thickness, scramblers grow at a great rate, and are excellent producers of flowers and fruit. This makes scramblers very decorative in cultivation, provided that a good position can be found. Not all gardeners like the way scramblers grow naturally, sprawling over everything else. However, they can be grown in suitable places – a dead tree makes a good base for a scrambler, as does a bare fence. In both cases, the scrambler has an opportunity denied to it in the wild – a constant, high degree of support and light. It responds by producing extra leaves, and quickly hides the fence and makes a good screen. Scramblers can be mixed in a boundary screen, where they will help to bind the shrubbery together. Such a living wall is difficult to penetrate, even if no spiny plants are used. Scramblers will also grow well on a pergola.

### *Propagation*

Nearly all indigenous shrubs are best grown from seed. Soft-wooded species, such as *Adenia* and *Aloe*, are exceptions – they should be grown from cuttings. Unless otherwise stated, all seeds need much the same treatment. The seeds should normally be separated from the rest of the fruit, whether they are to be planted or stored. This is especially important in the case of soft fruits, which rapidly become mouldy, the fungus then killing the seeds. Alternatively, the moisture retained by soft fruit may be enough to trigger germination before the seed is planted in a suitable bed.

If seed is going to be stored, it must be kept dry, as it will remain inert in this state. In the wild this enables it to survive difficult conditions for some time. Indeed, a number of species have a compulsory dormant period, which ensures that they germinate at the best time. Dormancy provides the seed with insurance against extinction during drought or cold. Some species display intermittent germination, which means that not all the seeds in one batch will germinate at the same time, even when the perfect conditions are provided. The significance of this is that the seeds cannot be 'fooled' into all germinating at once by the first wetting, since the moisture provided by one brief shower may well not be enough to establish the seedling properly.

- **Plant your seed right away** All species of shrub seeds are best planted right away, for their viability will always diminish with age. The seeds of some shrub species are worthless after as little as three days. Germination commences once the right combination of water, oxygen and warmth is provided. The ideal combination is not known for most indigenous plants, and germination times vary a lot. Consequently, the trick is not to give up too soon. There are some seeds that also require light in order to germinate. This is generally true of small seeds that do not have sufficient inner food resources to sustain growth away from sunlight. They are also vulnerable to fungal attack if they are left in the shade. Larger seeds (ones that are approximately 1 cm long) are designed to germinate in partial shade, the resulting seedling remaining almost dormant until sunlight penetrates a gap in the forest canopy, causing it to spring suddenly to life. However, under nursery conditions such large seeds will germinate perfectly well given light. Even though they have their own food stores to sustain them in the shade, the extra energy from the sunlight will certainly not go amiss. Germination can sometimes be speeded up if you make sure that the seed gets the right pre-treatment. This usually involves weakening the resistance of the seed coat, by abrasion, soaking in hot water, passage through the gut of a bird or mammal, or scorching in a fire.
- **Dealing with tough seeds** The best way of abrading seeds is to scrape them, one at a time, on sandpaper or a metal file. Hard seeds, especially larger ones, benefit from this. Such seeds also respond well to hot water treatment. To treat the seeds, put the ones that are not germinating in a basin and pour boiling water over them. Then leave them to soak for up to a day, until they swell. Wild birds are also great natural seed processors – you can copy their effect using the services of a tame turkey in a pen, where its droppings can easily be collected. Fire treatment, too, can help with tough seeds. This is best provided by piling dry grass over a heap of seeds and setting fire to it. By placing the seeds in a pile, you ensure there are some that get the optimum scorch, whether they are on the outside or the inside of the heap.

### *Planting seeds*

Plant the fresh or treated seeds in a seed bed, at a depth equal to their own size. A seed bed contains a germinating medium of 50% finely milled pine bark, 25% sand and 25% compost. A 15-cm layer of this is adequate, if good drainage is provided by an underlying layer of coarse gravel and broken bricks. Enclose the bed with a low wall to keep out all other plants. Keep the seeds damp, but not sodden, and do not give up too quickly – several species take up to a year to germinate. The seed bed should never be in full shade – keep it under 30% shade-cloth or under glass. In warmer areas seeds can be planted at any time of the year, but avoid winter planting in colder areas.

Once they have grown their first few leaves, seedlings can be potted in the same mixture used in the seed bed, or a mixture of equal parts topsoil, sand and compost. Never use just garden soil, as it cakes solid and roots are unable to develop. Moreover, it is often full of weed seeds. Hold the seedling, roots dangling, with one hand, and fill the container around it until all roots are covered. This way they are arranged in a natural position and do not get damaged. Press the potting medium down by hand so that the seedling stands upright without support. Water sparingly and regularly, until the plant is established. Do not plant tiny seedlings directly into the garden; they dry out too quickly, and may even not be found again among larger plants.

### *Cuttings*

Many shrubs grow easily from stem or tip cuttings, and you can use this method for plants whose seed is unobtainable, or for ones that take better from cuttings (as

**TOP:** *Senecio tamoides*
**MIDDLE:** *Hibiscus tiliaceus*
**ABOVE:** *Ochna natalitia*

detailed in the entry for each shrub, under 'Propagation'). Cuttings are best taken in July and August if you live in a warm area. Mid-September is better in cooler areas. Tip cuttings generally work best with soft-wooded plants. Cut a section long enough to include four nodes – a node being the section between adjoining leaves. For hardwood cuttings discard the soft terminal growth altogether; the cutting must consist of last year's, or even older, hard wood. Again, four nodes' length is ideal.

- **How to take a good cutting** A clean cut with a sharp implement is essential. Ragged cuts will fray, usually leading to rot. It is important to work fast, since cuttings rapidly dry out. Plunge fresh cuttings instantly into water or wrap them in wet newspaper, as a plant is essentially a pump, and the entry of air bubbles will block its water passage. Succulent cuttings are the exception; they do better if allowed to dry for a few days in a dry shady spot until a callus forms over the cut surface. Roots will then sprout from this. Rooting hormone can be applied to the cut end before planting; it tends to make very little difference in warmer climates, but it can improve success in cooler areas.

Cuttings sometimes root if stuck straight into the ground, but, to avoid damaging the cutting, make the hole with a blunt stick rather than with the base of the cutting. Put two nodes into the hole, leaving two sticking out. Chances are improved if they are started in river sand, especially if a mist-bed is available. In a mist-bed, which must be housed under glass to retain humidity, a pre-programmed automatic water-sprayer delivers a fine mist at frequent intervals over the cuttings. Without a mist-bed, water sparingly and often. Trim off all, or most of, the leaves on a new cutting, for without roots it cannot supply enough water to all its leaves. New cuttings like shelter; use either glass or 50% shade-cloth.

- **Cuttings from roots made easy** Root cuttings (sections of root simply cut into 20-cm sections), buried 2–3 cm deep in river sand, work best for some shrub species; *Carissa tetramera* is a good example. Make sure you keep the sand damp, as for stem cuttings. Whatever the type of cutting, the time to transplant it to an individual pot is when new leaves sprout. Check to see if roots are at least 2 cm long (if not, just wait for them to grow a little more). If so, replant cuttings exactly as though they were seedlings, and subsequent treatment should be the same too.

### Preparing a hole and planting

The ideal time to plant out is in spring, as soon as the last winter frost is safely past. This allows the longest possible time for the young shrub to grow before cold weather next stops growth. Roots begin growing once the weather starts warming up; growth is retarded if the roots are cramped in a pot.

It is vital to give a shrub the best possible start. It has already cost money or effort, and will give great pleasure for years to come. Moreover, if it is a rare or unusual species, it may be impossible to replace later. So do not skimp on preparing the hole. The absolute minimum size for a planting hole, in good soil, is 60 cm square; a 1-m hole is needed in poor soil. Put the topsoil in one heap, the subsoil in another. The difference between the two is usually obvious, subsoil often being coarser and stonier, or consisting of solid clay, while topsoil always has a lighter feel and contains finely fragmented leaf litter. Discard any big stones.

- **Home soil** There are a few shrub species that seem to need some soil from the areas where they are found naturally, growing painfully slowly without it. They probably depend upon a vital micro-organism in the soil. The only foolproof way to ensure you have the right soil is to take some from the base of a wild shrub of the same species (taking soil from nearby areas, even if they are within the shrub's overall general range, will not help). Incorporate this soil from the shrub's natural range into the topsoil heap that will be used to fill the hole.
- **Drainage and filling** Test drainage by filling the hole with water. If it drains away very slowly then abandon that spot, unless you are planting a swamp-loving shrub. If all is well, fill the hole, mixing the soil in a 3:1 ratio with compost or completely rotted manure. Then, put the topsoil in the bottom of the hole (where it will be of most use). The only extra fertiliser you will need is a handful each of superphosphate and 2.3.2, which you should mix into the soil that is already in the hole.
- **Planting the shrub** Fill the hole, gently treading the mixture down, to the point where the shrub – still in its container – sits in the hole at the desired height. Remove the shrub for the moment. Now fill the hole with water, and allow it to drain away. Do this at least six times so that the original hole and its surrounds are completely sodden. Carefully remove the plant from its container, making sure not to disturb the ball of soil holding the roots. Place the shrub and soil ball in the hole. If it leans naturally, tilt the soil ball until the stem is vertical; this is much better than staking the shrub later. Then fill the rest of the hole with the soil mixture and water once more. Place a mulch around the plant, on the wet soil, to reduce evaporation.

### Post-planting care

Except in unusual circumstances, such as severe drought, never water the shrub again. However, in an emergency, leave a finely trickling hose at the shrub base for several hours: never, never use a bucket or watering can. If a shrub was properly watered initially, there should now be enough water beneath the shrub to last for weeks, at least until the next rain. In dry weather, soil water moves upwards, so the shrub's roots will always be in contact with damp soil. Moreover, a degree of drought resistance can be instilled into any plant by growing it in dry conditions. Such plants have smaller leaf cells and a thicker cuticle. So do not pamper a young shrub if drought is to be a perpetual problem. If it overcomes a dry period shortly after planting, it is likely to withstand drought reliably thereafter. Subsequent superficial watering is actually counter-productive, since it encourages growth of surface roots at the expense of deeper-growing roots that secure the shrub's future. Shrubs with surface roots are much more likely to be blown over, and will continually suffer water-stress, necessitating endless watering. If a shrub droops, let it droop. If it dies, plant something more suitable for your garden's particular conditions next time.

### *Weeding*

Large weeds threatening a small shrub need removing, but be very careful around proteas and their relatives. These plants have vital and very delicate surface roots, which can be easily destroyed if you yank out a large, nearby weed. Such weeds must be cut back carefully, and not uprooted. Ideally, you should plant a shallow-rooted grass (most grasses, except for kikuyu) around proteas, and keep it neatly mown.

### *Pruning*

Prune with restraint. More than a few plants produce flowers and fruit only on their newest growth. Pruning may suppress this flowering and fruiting altogether. Constantly pruning a plant because it gets too big means that the wrong species was chosen in the first place. Start again with something smaller. However, some shrubs do need regular pruning to maintain vigour; *Leonotis* is a good example. Typically, these are species that get burnt or frosted back in the wild each year. Check the subject's wild growth habits before taking action. Pruning a leading shoot shifts action of the growth hormone in a plant. When the leading shoot is gone, axillary buds (those dormant at the base of the leaves) start to grow vigorously, producing new branches near ground level. Where some pruning is required, whether to remove long branches, or to bush up the lower stem (by removing the leading shoot, as described above), it should be done in a way that does not spoil the natural outline of the plant. Cut the branch(es) back to a point deep inside the canopy. Then, any new growth from this point will have assumed an irregular shape by the time it emerges.

Pruning rules differ in the *Protea* family. Both *Protea* and *Leucadendron* benefit greatly from regular pruning. Behead the plant when it reaches a height of 40 cm, and regularly cut the taller branches until the plant is five years old or so, by which time it should be very bushy. Always make sure that you cut well above the lowest leaves on a branch: new growth will come only from buds in the axils of those leaves.

### *Using chemicals*

In a word: don't. Indigenous shrubs never die from an attack by insects. Let a plague run its course. Chemicals kill birds, lizards and many other friendly creatures in your garden, without ever eliminating the target pest totally. Should a shrub appear permanently stricken, you should replace it with something more suitable, as opposed to using chemicals that can harm birds and other animals.

## Creating a bird, bat and butterfly garden

Nearly all gardeners enjoy the company of birds. Birds are however more than aesthetic dressing – they are great environmental indicators, their presence paying tribute to a garden's quality. In any garden there will be factors limiting bird numbers and diversity. Usually, the main problem is shortage of nest sites, followed by shortage of natural food (mainly insects) and cover. This explains why a bird table with the traditional offering of breadcrumbs is successful only to a point. The real task is to address the things reducing bird numbers and diversity in your garden, and to provide different habitats and resources. The same principle applies to catering for bats, and especially butterflies, that depend upon particular plant species.

### *Structuring your garden*

The complete reconstruction of natural habitats is not essential to attracting birds and other animals. However, the general structure of your garden is very important; it must copy the irregularity of most wild habitats. The simplest 'natural' garden to create is a 'bushveld' one. This typically has open areas, and its most important plants are bushes and small trees. These may be scattered, but are often clumped, sometimes into thickets. So shrubs are the most useful plants in a wildlife garden, as their structure appeals to lots of birds. Most shrubs branch frequently, maximising both hiding places for invertebrates, and perches from which small birds can look for them. Shrubs offer cover, and security for nest sites near ground level. True bushveld plants are not essential in a bird garden; more important is to use plants best suited to the local climate and soil conditions.

Plant around the garden's boundaries. In nature much wildlife action occurs along habitat edges, so try to maximise the amount of 'edge' in the garden. To do this, pack plants along property boundaries and have winding strips or clumps elsewhere. This arrangement also offers the best opportunity for viewing animals.

### *Natural food supply*

With few exceptions, indigenous plants provide much more food (directly and indirectly) for local animals and insects than aliens. This is particularly true when it comes to the invertebrates required by insectivorous birds, and by nestlings of nearly all bird species. Indigenous plants, especially those occurring naturally close to you, have evolved over a long period together with the insects with which they coexist, and so support far more than an alien plant which has only just arrived (most within just the last 100 years or so, while these adaptations take in the region of at least 10,000 years). Indigenous plants are also more reliable fruit-producers, as their local specialised pollinating agents (that is, local insects!) are present.

### *Good shrubs for attracting insects*

The smaller insects enjoyed by robins, shrikes and warblers tend to concentrate on white flowers with an

TOP: *Psychotria capensis*
MIDDLE: Green pigeon
ABOVE: *Putterlickia verrucosa*

appreciable smell, which almost all of them have. These flowers need not be large and showy, indeed many of them are small, although produced in masses. Nor need the smell be sweet, although often it is: musty smells also attract insects. Other shrubs, such as figs, attract insects with their soft fruits, especially as these become over-ripe. Clouds of fruit-flies swarm to the fruits and are the target of flycatchers. Shrubs with edible foliage, such as *Clausena*, are periodically inundated with caterpillars. Small cryptically-coloured caterpillars are eaten by most birds, but the hairy types are the favourite food of orioles and cuckoos. Many insects and other invertebrates are also attracted to rough-barked shrubs, especially species that have loose, overlapping layers of bark. Spiders, mantises and other predatory insects lurk here, and many other species pupate under the comparative security of loose bark. Their hiding places are constantly searched by woodpeckers, barbets, woodhoopoes and black tits. *Lycium* has insect-friendly bark.

Another important source of insects, especially to birds such as thrushes and robins, is the leaf-litter layer. Always leave leaf-litter in shady spots, where there is little or nothing growing.

### Good flowering shrubs for attracting birds

Flowers that attract birds are usually red and tubular, with a pool of nectar at the bottom, like those of *Aloe*. Birds stick their heads right into the tube, using their long, thin bills to reach the nectar. As they do so they collect some pollen on their heads. This is then deposited in the next flower when the bird moves on. Each flower produces a succession of florets, ensuring continuity of nectar production, so that birds return every day. The sunbirds and sugarbirds attracted to these displays are the most spectacular of all garden visitors. The different species of red-flowering shrubs have their own flowering season, between them filling the calendar, so use as many as possible.

### Bird-attracting fruiting shrubs

Birds also assist in plant dispersal, and fleshy fruits are the reward for transporting seeds. A practical way to choose a fruiting shrub is to observe which species prove attractive in the surrounding veld. Otherwise, find out whether a chosen shrub will produce fruit in your particular area. Being 'indigenous' does not guarantee fruiting, particularly if the shrub's naturally range is in a distant, different climatic region where its only pollinators live.

Many bird-dispersed berries are red or shiny black. Berry-bearing shrubs usually first fruit at two to three years, and are essential in a new garden where near-instant results are wanted. They are suitable for any omnivore. For best results plant a variety of fruiting shrubs, rather than concentrating on one prolific species. Choosing species which fruit at different times may induce fruit-eating birds to stay almost throughout the year. Of course this plan may still fail if only the male of a single-sexed shrub is planted (male shrubs do not produce fruit). If space permits, always plant two or more of any such species to maximise your chances of planting a female; otherwise play safe and use bisexual shrubs.

### Good nesting shrubs

An average garden might be used by as many as 50 bird species, but only a very few will nest there. This is because birds are much fussier about their choice of nesting site than they are about food. Spiny shrubs are the favourite nesting sites of small birds. Spines provide a good anchorage for the nest itself, and are a great deterrent to any predator, including domestic cats, which are highly efficient killers.

Scramblers are also a great asset in a wildlife garden. They link adjacent shrubs, creating access routes for animals. They provide much food for birds and insects, but are especially important as nesting sites. Any thick, tangled vegetation makes a good hiding place, but scramblers have an extra property, which provides greater security: by holding on to everything, including its own branches and trunk, a scrambler's branches form a long-lasting network that resists storms and other calamities, which would otherwise tear birds' nests apart.

### Creating a butterfly-friendly garden

Each butterfly species lays its eggs on a favourite host plant, as emerging caterpillars are very fussy about diet. You should provide these food plants (see entries marked with the butterfly symbol) in your garden in order to attract butterflies. A successful hatch can reduce a shrub to something resembling a string vest. However, once all the leaves are eaten, the caterpillars must die or pupate. Their highly precise digestion forbids them to shift to a different species of plant. After a short pause, the shrub will then grow a complete set of new leaves. The best place to create a butterfly garden is on a ridge or hilltop. Territorial males prefer such spots where their displays can best be seen, attracting more females. Population dispersal of butterflies also tends to be via hilltops.

### Encouraging bats

Bats occur throughout the country and in every habitat, so all gardens already have them whether their owners realise it or not. Several things can be done to improve conditions for bats. First, maintain an eco-friendly garden. The majority of our bats are insect-eaters, and so respond to the quantity and quality of nocturnal insect life. Second, maintain roost sites in your garden. Many bats roost in hollow trunks or branches of big dead trees, or under large pieces of loose bark. Some also depend upon particular shrubs for roosting. *Strelitzia nicolai* is a good example of a special bat roost.

# HOW TO USE THIS BOOK

The feature below explains each aspect of the shrub entries, and the symbols used in the book are explained in the key, to the right. This key is repeated on the very last page of the book (page 112) for quick-reference. Consult the glossary on the same page for further help.

❶ **Hibiscus tiliaceus**

❷ Lagoon hibiscus

❸ 

❹ **Size:** 3–6 x 4–9 m (wild), up to 4 x 6 m (garden)

❺ **Natural habitat:** *H. tiliaceus* is found naturally on the coast, from about East London northwards. It invariably occurs in estuaries, where it may form a dense fringe just above the high-tide mark, and in swamp forests.

❻ **Growth form:** It is multi-stemmed, the branches forming a dense tangle. The leaves are very handsome, large and heart-shaped, with a greyish tinge. The flowers too are outstanding, large, bright pale yellow, later turning orange or even red before they fall. The centre of the flower is deep maroon. The seeds are dispersed by water, floating naturally for six months and more.

❼ **Propagation:** Seed. Harvest it just before the mature dry fruit splits, scattering the lot. Cuttings strike easily.

❽ **Uses:** *H. tiliaceus* makes a striking if unconventional specimen, given enough space, and is particularly attractive next to water. It is one of the fastest growing indigenous shrubs, achieving up to 2 m per year initially. Flowering begins in the second year. It also makes an impenetrable screen. *H. tiliaceus* thrives on or near the southeastern coast, but need not be planted in a damp spot. Inland it languishes through droughts and must be given a wet sunny position.

**Hoslundia opposita**

Orange bird-berry

**Size:** 1–2 x 1–2 m (wild), up to 1 x 1 m (garden)

**Natural habitat:** *Hoslundia* ranges from the warmer parts of much of the east to the south coast of KwaZulu-Natal. It grows in grassland and open woodland.

**Growth form:** There are two growth forms; an upright form, better for the small garden, and the creeping form from Zululand. *Hoslundia* is evergreen with dense foliage. Leaves are pale green and, like other members of the mint family, have a crisp smell when crushed. The flowers are minute but attractive to butterflies. Chameleons often lie in ambush just under the flower heads. The soft orange 'fruits' are actually swollen calyxes. They glow in contrast with the foliage. *Hoslundia* is one of the best bird-attracting fruits of all, much loved by bulbuls.

**Propagation:** Seed. Semi-hardwood cuttings also root easily.

**Uses:** *Hoslundia* makes a perfect foliage and fruiting specimen for a small garden. Plant several around a bird bath: the dense mat of intertwined branches prevents cats from attacking birds. It can be regularly cut back, but never remove more than a quarter of the foliage at once. *Hoslundia* grows to full size within two years. It likes a warm summer with at least moderate rainfall.

❾ **Make your own compost** Every garden should have a corner where compost can be made. Use vegetable peelings and fruit waste from the kitchen, weeds, and soft, spent plants. The addition of animal manure will speed up the decomposition process.

62

❶ The shrub's newest scientific name (check the index, page 110, for old scientific names)

❷ The best-known common name(s) for the shrub

❸ Symbols showing the shrub's characteristics, and the conditions in which it grows best, at a glance (see the key to the right)

❹ Size the shrub reaches in the wild, followed by the size it grows to in the garden

❺ The area(s) where the shrub is found naturally, in the wild

❻ The way the shrub typically develops – its main characteristics, such as shape, foliage, fruit and flowers

❼ How you can go about growing the shrub (see the Introduction, pages 5 and 6, for details on propagation)

❽ The best uses for the shrub in the garden, and the climate and conditions in which it will grow best

❾ Interesting information about indigenous shrubs and tips on how best to garden with them

## SYMBOLS

 Grows best in full sun

 Grows best in partial shade

 Grows best in shade

 Deciduous shrub (loses its leaves)

 Evergreen shrub (never loses its leaves)

 Scrambler (no thick trunk, grows over surrounding vegetation)

 Flowers are an attractive feature

 Fruit is an attractive feature

 Attracts butterflies

 Attracts birds

 Attracts bats

 Grows well in clay

 Survives severe drought

 Survives moderate drought

 Grows well in coastal sand and withstands coastal wind

 Grows in waterlogged soil

 Survives harsh frost

 Survives moderate frost

 Survives light frost

**No frost symbol:** Cannot survive frost

 Grows best in area with high rainfall

 Grows best in area with moderate rainfall

 Grows best in area with low rainfall

## Abrus precatorius

### Abrus

**Size:** 2–8 m long (wild), up to 6 m long (garden)
**Natural habitat:** *Abrus* grows naturally from the Eastern Cape through KwaZulu-Natal's coastal plain to the eastern Lowveld. It occurs in dry woodland, nearly always at the edge of small thickets.
**Growth form:** It is a modest but thorny scrambler, with sparse foliage. Its small pink flowers are pretty, though short-lived, and *Abrus* only attracts serious attention when it fruits. The fruits are small pods, clustered together, that split when ripe. Each cluster looks like an untidy cardboard mobile, up to 10 cm in diameter, with brilliant red-and-black seeds protruding from every opening. They hang for months like superior Christmas decorations, illuminating their support.
**Propagation:** Seed.
**Uses:** *Abrus* must be planted against a support – a trellis or a shrubby tree will do. Fruits are produced during the first year, and make such a lovely display that they should get a prime spot. If picked when fully ripe and dry they last for years as ornaments, but handle with care later; the seeds fall out easily. Growth rate is modest by scrambler standards, about 1 m per year. *Abrus* has so far been grown only in a warm climate. It is unlikely to tolerate frost.

## Acacia ataxacantha

### Flame thorn

**Size:** 10–30 m long (wild), up to 15 m long (garden)
**Natural habitat:** This species is found naturally in most of the east. It occurs in a variety of wooded habitats, particularly in tall thickets, and even in mist-belt forest.
**Growth form:** In the wild it is always a rambling shrub, its long branches climbing through surrounding vegetation, their many hooked thorns grasping every support. Leaves are finely divided into hundreds of tiny leaflets. *A. ataxacantha* is noted for both flowering and fruiting displays. The flowers are long white sweet-smelling brushes that occur in late summer, attracting many small insects and insectivorous birds. Autumn sees brilliant red, hanging pods.
**Propagation:** Seed. Older seeds germinate better if scarified and soaked in hot water before planting.
**Uses:** This shrub's straggly nature makes it an excellent boundary barrier. In full sunlight it retains most of its foliage on the lower branches, making a visual screen, while the thorns eagerly grasp the fence, other plants and intruders. Flowering begins at three years. Growth is rapid, at least 1 m per year without support, but two to three times as much against a fence or nearby shrub. *A. ataxacantha* likes a warm summer but otherwise tolerates almost any climatic extreme.

**Decorative seeds** Collect some seeds of *Abrus precatorius* when you're in the bush and put them in a container – they look wonderfully decorative.

## Acokanthera oppositifolia

**Bushman's poison**

**Size:** 2–5 x 2–5 m (wild), up to 5 x 5 m (garden)
**Natural habitat:** This species extends from the southern Cape through most of the east and north of the country. It is usually found in thick deciduous woodland.
**Growth form:** *Acokanthera* is an upright shrub with craggy bark. The leaves are dark, thick, leathery and handsome. Strongly scented white flowers with a pink tinge occur in early spring. The fruits are large fleshy berries, initially red, turning black. The entire fruit crop is always eaten, mature fruits being ripped to pieces by birds until eventually only the translucent pips remain.
**Propagation:** Seed.
**Uses:** *Acokanthera* makes a fine small foliage and flower specimen, a good screen, and is ideal in a bird garden. A fruit-bearing branch lasts for weeks in a cut flower arrangement. Flowering and fruiting begin at three years. Growth rate is about 50 cm per year. It grows in almost any climate, although it prefers moderate rainfall and a warm summer. This shrub grows well in a container, tolerating poor light and air-conditioning for long spells indoors. This plant has a fearsome reputation amongst the San (Bushmen) as a source of poison. It is certainly toxic, but perfectly safe to touch.

## Acridocarpus natalitius

**Moth-fruit**

**Size:** 1–4 x 1–3 m (wild), up to 3 x 2 m (garden)
**Natural habitat:** *Acridocarpus* is found naturally on the Eastern Cape and KwaZulu-Natal coasts. It is common in lowland forest and also occurs on krans edges.
**Growth form:** Usually it is a small spindly shrub in the gloom of the forest floor, but it transforms if given light. In the open it tends to stay shrubby, but thickens out, or becomes a scrambler in a forest clearing. Mature trunks have thick bark that develops winged ridges. The leaves are dark and glossy, the surface being slightly puckered, creating a quilted appearance. The attractive bright yellow flowers are quite large, and are borne in upright spikes. Carpenter bees like them. The fruit has two papery wings and is said to resemble a moth. Butterflies of the family Hesperiidae breed on *Acridocarpus*.
**Propagation:** Seed.
**Uses:** It makes a beautiful flowering, fruiting and foliage shrub. First flowering occurs at three years. Speed of growth depends on the availability of support. Without it, growth rate is about 40 cm per year. Alternatively, *Acridocarpus* can be planted against a fence, and branches will grow 1 m and more per year. It must have a warm summer with good rainfall, and cannot stand drought or frost.

**Forest** A forest is a naturally occurring community of trees in which the canopy is closed. It need not be evergreen, but usually is in South Africa. A forest is a 'climax community', unique in that it is the end-product of a series of vegetation changes, and won't change further. It is always found where water is abundant and grass fires never penetrate.

## Adenia gummifera

**Wild granadilla**

**Size:** 8–30 m long (wild), up to 17 m long (garden)
**Natural habitat:** *Adenia* is restricted to the coastal forests of the Eastern Cape and KwaZulu-Natal.
**Growth form:** It is a vigorous creeper, using tendrils to scale the tallest tree. Its most obvious attraction is its trunk. This is smooth, almost oily, and bright pale green, longitudinally striped white, and could quite easily pass as a giant snake. The leaves are very soft and lobed like those of a maple. The flowers are insignificant, but the fruits are small green balloons that can make a pleasant display.
**Propagation:** Cuttings. Seed has not yet been tried.
**Uses:** *Adenia* makes an intriguing accent plant for a larger garden. The beauty of the trunk is apparent at two years, and fruiting begins at four. It must be grown against a strong fence or over a large pergola. It is even worth ring-barking and killing an expendable tree to accommodate *Adenia*. The foliage is too sparse to provide a screen. Growth is rapid, at least 3 to 4 m per year once the plant is established. It likes a warm summer, with good rainfall. Frost-hardiness is likely to be nil, and *Adenia* has yet to be tested in a dry environment.

## Adenium multiflorum

**Impala lily**

**Size:** 1–3 x 1–3 m (wild), up to 3 x 3 m (garden)
**Natural habitat:** This species is confined to Zululand and the Lowveld, where it occurs on hot rocky slopes.
**Growth form:** The impala lily is a fat, silvery-barked succulent with a few stubby branches. It may be leafless for up to six months, during which time the plant may be easily overlooked as a rock. Wild specimens are often nibbled by antelopes down to ground level. In winter it produces dazzling flowers – white stars framed with red. These are followed by fruits that resemble pairs of ox-horns. They split when mature, releasing seeds that are each carried by a parachute.
**Propagation:** Seed or cuttings. Good drainage, as well as full sunlight are essential. Once established it needs extra water only when the trunk shrinks.
**Uses:** The impala lily is the most striking of all succulents. Many are planted in Kruger Park tourist camps where they grow to be huge. They like north-facing rockeries or life in a large tub, but must have a warm summer and a dry, frost-free winter. Flowering is then reliable, but fruiting does not take place outside the natural range. Flowering begins at two years, but it will not flower in the shade. Growth is slow, rarely more than 20 cm per year.

**Townhouse gardens** If you live in a flat or small townhouse you can still enjoy indigenous gardening. Many indigenous shrubs flourish in pots and, like any other plants, will thrive if given enough light and air. *Acokanthera oppositifolia*, *Adenium multiflorum* and *Dermatobotrys saundersii* are ideal species to grow in pots.

## Alberta magna

### Natal flame bush, Alberta

**Size:** 3–6 x 3–6 m (wild), up to 4 x 4 m (garden)
**Natural habitat:** *Alberta* has a restricted distribution in the Eastern Cape and the KwaZulu-Natal Midlands. It tends to occur on the edges of mist-belt forests and also on steep, grassy slopes amongst rocks.
**Growth form:** It is small and rounded, nearly always shrubby, with bold, glossy foliage. The flowers are brilliant red curved tubes arranged in bunches and appear in midsummer. Flowering continues until autumn, overlapping the fruiting period. The fruits are also bright red and have narrow, papery wings that persist on the tree for many weeks.
**Propagation:** Seed collected from wild plants very rarely germinates, but better results are obtained if seed from garden specimens is used. *Alberta* can be grown from cuttings.
**Uses:** This shrub is magnificent in cultivation, provided that the initial hurdle of germination can be overcome. It demands a prime position in the garden, and is wasted anywhere else. Growth is slow, at best 30 cm per year. However, the first flowering occurs in two or three years. *Alberta* likes fairly high rainfall and a temperate summer. It tolerates a cool summer, however, provided that winter has at most slight frost. It does not do well in Johannesburg, nor on the sub-tropical coast.

## Allophylus dregeanus

### One-leaf allophylus

**Size:** 3–5 x 3–4 m (wild), up to 4 x 4 m (garden)
**Natural habitat:** *A. dregeanus* is found in the Eastern Cape and KwaZulu-Natal. It occurs in evergreen forests, especially in the undergrowth and on the margins.
**Growth form:** It is small and can be upright, but tends to be shrubby. The leaves are glossy and neatly edged, and are eaten by caterpillars of the beautiful butterfly *Charaxes varanes*. The flowers are small and white, forming attractive masses. The main attraction of this shrub is its fruits – red berries, borne in hanging strings. Initially green, they turn red in sequence, starting at the bottom of the string. However, rarely is the sequence of colour-change observed because birds strip the ripe fruits off almost as soon as they redden.
**Propagation:** Seed.
**Uses:** *A. dregeanus* is well worth its place in a bird garden and is a useful filler in a forest clump. Speed of growth is about 50 cm per year, but first fruiting can be expected at three years or even earlier. Note that fruit production has not been seen outside the natural range. It grows best where rainfall is moderate to good, and the summer temperate to warm. It survives an average winter drought and slight frost.

**Staggered flowering** The flowering seasons of plants bearing red flowers are staggered so that only one indigenous species of red flower peaks in an area at a time. This ensures that pollinating birds transfer pollen to the correct species.

## Allophylus natalensis

**Dune allophylus**

**Size:** 3–5 x 4–6 m (wild), up to 3 x 4 m (garden)
**Natural habitat:** This is a coastal species, which it extends from East London northwards. While it is common in dune forest, it is quite rare elsewhere.
**Growth form:** *A. natalensis* is always shrubby, whether forming a stunted canopy on the seaward side of the dune, or part of the undergrowth of more sheltered places. The leaves are attractive, with well-marked veins and neatly serrate edges. They are the food of caterpillars of the butterfly *Charaxes varanes*. *A. natalensis* has white flowers which, although small, are borne in massed spikes in early winter, producing a pleasant scent and attracting many insects. They are followed by red berries tightly clustered along slender branchlets.
**Propagation:** Seed.
**Uses:** *A. natalensis* is especially useful at the coast because it resists sea breezes. It can be used as a windbreak initially, and is worth retaining as a decorative shrub and for birds once the garden is established. The berries make a stunning show in late winter, but fruit production has not been noted outside the natural habitat. Speed of growth is about 50 cm per year, and first fruiting can be expected at three years or even earlier. It tolerates moderate drought.

## Aloe arborescens

**Krantz aloe**

**Size:** 2–3 x 3–4 m (wild), up to 3 x 3 m (garden)
**Natural habitat:** *A. arborescens* ranges from the southwestern Cape through the wetter regions of the country to the eastern Escarpment. It occurs on rock outcrops, krans edges and other exposed spots protected from fire.
**Growth form:** It is a succulent. Although single-stemmed it branches low down, forming a dense shrub. The leaves are toothed, curved and glossy, and arranged in perfect rosettes. The spectacular flowers appear in autumn and last until mid-winter. They are typical of *Aloe*, red and tubular, maturing in sequence on a series of vertical spikes.
**Propagation:** Cuttings. Almost any broken-off piece of stem will root, even if just stuck into unprepared ground. Seed will germinate easily, but can be collected only by encasing growing fruits with gauze before they explode.
**Uses:** It provides accent in a dry flowerbed or rockery, as well as being pretty in its own right. The flowers are certain to bring sunbirds, so plant *A. arborescens* near the stoep where the birds can be watched at leisure. Flowering begins at two years. *A. arborescens* likes almost any climate, but cannot stand severe frost. Moderate frost may cut down the flowering spikes without affecting the parent plant.

**Avoid moving shrubs** Careful initial planning of planting positions will save you from having to transplant your shrubs later on. As a rule of thumb, shrubs don't like being moved and often take a long time to flourish again.

## Andrachne ovalis

**False lightning bush**

**Size:** 1–4 x 1–4 m (wild), up to 3 x 3 m (garden)
**Natural habitat:** *Andrachne* ranges from the southern Cape east and north up to the eastern Escarpment. It is confined to evergreen forests, and is sometimes found on the margins, but more often in the deep interior.
**Growth form:** It is usually a much-branched rounded bush. It is evergreen with a soft, slightly weeping appearance. The flowers are insignificant, but the fruits are pretty. They are three-lobed capsules that hang on long stalks in rows. They mature to yellow before splitting to release the seeds.
**Propagation:** Seed.
**Uses:** *Andrachne* has the merit of being one of the few shrubs that actually enjoys life in the shade. It makes a good filler in an unpopular shady spot, and an eye-level screen beneath tall trees. However, it grows well enough in full sun in a damp temperate climate. Fruiting begins in the second year, sometimes when the plant is still in a pot. Growth rate is moderate, about 40 cm per year. It thrives in a warm or cool summer provided that rainfall is high: it is not suitable for a dry climate. Frost tolerance is slight.

## Anisodontea julii

**Mountain mallow**

**Size:** 1–2 x 1 m (wild), up to 3 x 2 m (garden)
**Natural habitat:** *Anisodontea* is found naturally on the slopes of the Drakensberg, although it is absent from the highest peaks. It occurs in the evergreen scrub that often precedes forest regrowth, and among rocks, where it is protected from fire and the worst of the frost.
**Growth form:** It is a slim upswept shrub with large maple-like leaves, and has wonderful displays of large pale pink flowers throughout the summer. These are open cups, with narrow stripes of deeper pink, pointing pollinators in the right direction.
**Propagation:** Seed.
**Uses:** In cultivation *Anisodontea* grows bigger and better than it does in the wild, as though rewarding the gardener for releasing it from the bondage of fire and competition with taller plants. It grows to its full height within a single season, thickening out thereafter. Flowering takes place in the first summer, and seed shed around the parent plant produces a thriving colony in the second year. So, replacements are always ready when the original plant dies after five years or so. *Anisodontea* tolerates a wide range of summer temperatures, and is fairly frost hardy. It likes at least moderate rainfall, but survives normal winter drought.

**'Borrowed' foliage** If your neighbour has a shrubbery on your shared boundary, use this as a 'borrowed landscape' and plant your garden to complement the existing shrubs. You will create the impression that your garden extends further than it does.

## Apodytes abbottii

### Pondo white pear

**Size:** 1–3 x 1–3 m (wild), up to 2 x 2 m (garden)
**Natural habitat:** This shrub is confined to the Pondoland sandstone around the Umtamvuna River. It has only just been described, despite being quite common on rock outcrops in grassland next to public footpaths in Umtamvuna Nature Reserve.
**Growth form:** *A. abbottii* is a small, stiff, rounded shrub with purple twigs and smart, circular leaves. It has small white sweet-smelling flowers, produced in massed, branched heads in late spring. These are followed by very distinctive fruits – flat, black berries held in place by red cups. These are almost certainly bird-dispersed.
**Propagation:** Seed.
**Uses:** *A. abbottii* makes a good miniature foliage and flowering specimen, and is ideal for a small garden. It is fairly slow-growing, about 40 cm per year, but flowering begins at two to three years. It prefers a temperate to warm climate with good rainfall, but tolerates an average winter drought, and was unmarked by a series of moderate frosts. Despite its apparent dependence upon poor sandy soil in the wild it thrives in shale, and seems very flexible in cultivation.

## Artabotrys monteiroae

### Red hook-berry

**Size:** 2–4 x 1–2 m (wild), up to 3 x 1 m (garden)
**Natural habitat:** This species of shrub is found in Zululand and in the Soutpansberg. It occurs on the fringes of riverine and sand forests and in thickets.
**Growth form:** *Artabotrys* is a multi-stemmed shrub with a strong tendency to scramble over other plants. It does so with its flower stalks, which form remarkable hooks. Sometimes these embed themselves in neighbours. The shrub's foliage is brilliantly glossy, and it has unusual white flowers that resemble hollow lanterns, borne in small bunches. They are followed by bright red berries, sought after by birds. Caterpillars of *Graphium* butterflies rely upon *Artabotrys*.
**Propagation:** Seed, which is very often spread and planted by a number of birds and mammals.
**Uses:** *Artabotrys* makes a lovely foliage specimen, and its hooks never fail to attract attention. Fruiting has not yet been seen outside the natural habitat. It is an ideal pergola plant, and scrambler along the edges of a garden. It is ideal for making the handles and framework of baskets because of its tough, twining ways. Growth rate is about 50 cm per year. It must have a warm summer with at least moderate rainfall.

**Pine needles** An acid mulch of pine needles is ideal for sandstone endemics (plants endemic to areas with much sandstone), such as *Apodytes abbottii* and *Maytenus bachmannii*. Pine mulch is easily obtained from a nearby plantation – but do ask permission.

## Asparagus falcatus

### Yellowwood asparagus

**Size:** up to 10 m long (wild), up to 6 m long (garden)
**Natural habitat:** *Asparagus* occurs in the warmer parts of the east and northeast. It is found in rocky woodlands, riverine vegetation and in drier coastal forest, notably around St Lucia.
**Growth form:** This shrub is a thorny climber with a deceptively delicate air. The thorns are small, but hooked and strong. The leaves are glossy and narrow, almost needle-like, hence the comparison with the yellowwood. *Asparagus* has exceptionally beautiful flowers and fruit. Both can cover the plant. The flowers are white and sweetly scented; the bright red berries appear in mid-winter and are enjoyed by birds.
**Propagation:** Seed.
**Uses:** *Asparagus* develops into a multi-stemmed clump at one year and must then be planted out, otherwise the tendrils will grab everything within reach. It likes to spiral up tall, straight supports, never overwhelms a sturdy tree and adds texture to a canopy. It is also ideal for a pergola or fence, and is spiny enough to make an adequate barrier. Flowering and fruiting begin at two years though fruits are sparse outside the natural range. Growth rate is at least 2 m per year. So far *Asparagus* has been tested only in frost-free gardens with good rainfall and warm summers.

## Azima tetracantha

### Needle bush

**Size:** 1–4 x 1–4 m (wild), up to 2 x 4 m (garden)
**Natural habitat:** It is found naturally in a broad coastal strip from the southern Cape to KwaZulu-Natal that extends into the eastern Lowveld. This shrub is found in woodland, often on termite mounds, but especially beside drainage lines or small pans in heavy clay soil.
**Growth form:** *Azima* is a dense, tangled shrub with green branches. Its most characteristic feature is its spines, which are long, straight and sharp, and always borne in sets of four at right angles to each other and the branch. The shrub bears white berries, reputedly edible, although scarcely tested.
**Propagation:** Seed.
**Uses:** This is hardly a pretty plant, although the dominance and repeated symmetry of the thorns do attract attention. It is a superb barrier plant, best used as a hedge. It can be encouraged to develop longer branches if sited against a fence. Growth rate is initially about 50 cm per year. Subsequently it will slow down but thicken out. It likes a warm summer, and can stand considerable drought, even during the growing season. Its performance in frost is not known.

**Pruning your climbers** Climbers and twiners should be pruned regularly. Check them every week in the growing season and make sure they are growing where and in the form you want them to.

## Barleria albostellata

### White barleria

**Size:** 1–2 x 1–2 m (wild), up to 2 x 2 m (garden)
**Natural habitat:** This is a very localised species, being restricted, in South Africa, to a couple of spots in the north-eastern Escarpment. It occurs in dry woodland on sandy soil.
**Growth form:** *B. albostellata* is a near-spherical shrub. Its foliage is very striking, the leaves being very furry and almost pure grey. The flowers are large and white, and clustered into heads. In midsummer they virtually cover the bush, and emphasise its rounded shape. The fruit is a hard flat capsule that remains buried in the dried flower head.
**Propagation:** Seed. As seed capsules turn brown they must be collected from the flower heads. If left any longer they split and the seeds are lost.
**Uses:** *B. albostellata* makes an exceptional flowering and foliage specimen. The leaf colour is ideal for a conventional garden adopting a grey theme. Small enough to be used in almost any garden, it also makes an adequate low screen. Flowering takes place in the first year, and the flowering season lasts at least five months. Growth is rapid, full size being attained in two to three years. It likes a warm summer and moderate rainfall and tolerates an average winter drought.

## Barleria rotundifolia

### Lowveld barleria

**Size:** 1–2 x 1–2 m (wild), up to 2 x 2 m (garden)
**Natural habitat:** *B. rotundifolia* is restricted to the Mpumalanga Lowveld, occurring naturally within the Nelspruit Botanic Gardens. It grows along rocky woodland watercourses.
**Growth form:** It is an upright shrub with dense, soft foliage, although closer contact reveals deception, as the plant bristles with thin sharp spines arranged in bunches along every branch. The flowers, which are borne for about six months from midsummer onwards, are outstanding. They are thin, yellow tubes, flaring unequally at the mouth, with four petals held high and vertically, and the fifth being lower and horizontal.
**Propagation:** Seed, but more than one parent clump is essential. Single plants are self-sterile (that is, they cannot fertilise themselves). Cuttings tend to be a bit temperamental to root, but harder wood is more successful than soft tips.
**Uses:** It makes a beautiful flowering specimen, and a good protective low hedge. It is ideal around birdbaths to ward off cats, without blocking the view. Small birds like nesting in *B. rotundifolia*, and it is a favourite and safe perch for lizards. It flowers in its first year, and grows to full size in its second. It must have a well-drained, sunny situation, and will not survive winter if its roots remain wet.

**Preparing for climbers and twiners** Have guide-wires ready to train climbers and twiners if they are not going to grow on a fence or trellis. If you do this, then the plant grows where you want it to, and you avoid unnecessary pruning and trimming later.

## Bauhinia bowkeri

**Kei bauhinia**

**Size:** 2–6 x 3–8 m (wild), up to 3 x 6 m (garden)
**Natural habitat:** This is a local endemic, being confined to a broad coastal strip from Port Elizabeth to the Kei River. It occurs in dense scrubby vegetation.
**Growth form:** It is an upright but spreading shrub. The leaves are partially cleft, resembling the footprint of a camel. The exotic *Bauhinia* gets its common name of 'camel's-foot' from this feature. The shape of the leaf is emphasised by its clearly defined veins. The flowers are large and white, the petals long, crinkled and clearly separated. The fruit is a woody pod.
**Propagation:** Seed. Germination of old seed is speeded by scarification and hot water treatment.
**Uses:** In cultivation this is a vigorous performer. It makes a good corner-filler, and the multi-stemmed growth form lends itself well to shrubberies and screens. It is also an attractive specimen, flowering prolifically and for long periods; individual flowers are long-lived. First flowering can be expected at two years. Vertical growth is at least 1 m per year initially, lateral growth considerably more. *B. bowkeri* likes a warm summer with moderate rainfall. It withstands a little frost.

## Bauhinia galpinii

**Pride-of-De Kaap**

**Size:** 3–5 x 5–12 m (wild), up to 5 x 10 m (garden)
**Natural habitat:** This species is a Lowveld inhabitant. It occurs in thickets on hot rocky slopes, especially near Barberton.
**Growth form:** This is a vigorous shrub, which scrambles if support is available, or sprawls if it is not. The leaves are partially cleft, resembling the footprint of a camel. *B. galpinii* is more or less evergreen, but thins a little in a severe winter. The flowers have brick-red spoon-shaped petals, and the intensity of their display makes it possible to identify the species from a considerable distance. The flowering period lasts six months or more. The butterflies *Charaxes jasius* and *Deudorix diocles* are dependent upon *B. galpinii.*
**Propagation:** Seed. Germination of old seed is speeded by scarification and hot water treatment.
**Uses:** *B. galpinii* is the ideal plant to fill an ugly corner or can be used as a wild hedge or flowering specimen if space is available. First flowering can generally be expected at two years. Growth is rampant if the climate is favourable, sometimes 2 m per year. It prefers a hot dry climate, but grows surprisingly well in wet areas. It can self-seed outside its natural range, technically becoming an invader in grassland, where control might be necessary.

**Birdbaths** Install at least two birdbaths in your garden. Site them where you can get the most enjoyment from watching the bathing antics of the birds. Clean the water regularly, and remember that many birds have short legs and so require shallow baths.

## Bauhinia natalensis

**Natal bauhinia**

**Size:** 1–2 x 1–2 m (wild), up to 2 x 2 m (garden)
**Natural habitat:** This dainty species occurs near the KwaZulu-Natal coast on steep rocky slopes.
**Growth form:** It is a smallish delicate shrub. The leaves are pretty, having the typical camel's-foot shape, yet in miniature. The flowers are white with simple oval petals. One petal has a red stripe up the centre, the two flanking petals have thinner, fainter stripes, the remaining two are plain white. The pattern acts as a signpost for pollinating insects. Flowering is profuse in spring, but a good display lasts for at least six months and a mature plant is seldom without a few flowers. Individual flowers are quite long-lived.
**Propagation:** Seed. Pods on garden specimens scatter seed, and a small colony will form around the parent plant within two to three years.
**Uses:** The combination of foliage and flowers makes *B. natalensis* an exceptional plant for any garden. It grows about 1 m per year, achieving almost full size at two years. Flowering starts at one year. Given a sunny position, it tolerates almost any rainfall, and although fairly sensitive to frost, its small size enables it to be planted close to a north-facing wall where it can avoid the worst.

## Bauhinia tomentosa

**Yellow tree bauhinia**

**Size:** 3–5 x 2–4 m (wild), up to 4 x 3 m (garden)
**Natural habitat:** This species occurs along the KwaZulu-Natal coast and the eastern Escarpment. It is found on forest edges and in thick low-growing scrub, particularly on sand dunes.
**Growth form:** *B. tomentosa* is a vigorous upright shrub. The branches are rather stiff, with the foliage all growing in one plane on any one branch. The leaves are partially cleft, resembling the footprint of a camel. The flowers are beautiful; pale yellow petals overlap around a maroon centre, and turn a veined purple with age.
**Propagation:** Seed. Germination of old seed is speeded by scarification and hot water treatment.
**Uses:** *B. tomentosa* is frequently used as a specimen because of its magnificent flowering, which lasts for most of the year. Individual flowers are long-lasting. The growth form lends itself well to shrubberies and screens. It grows over 1 m per year, and first flowering can be expected at two years. In some areas *B. tomentosa* appears prone to boring insects. Branches that die as a result need to be pruned off below the borer hole. *B. tomentosa* likes a warm summer but tolerates a wide rainfall range and can withstand some frost.

**Harvest new seedlings** Some shrubs produce lots of seedlings around the parent plant in a garden bed. Harvest some of these to transplant, or to give to friends. Examples are *Bauhinia natalensis, Polygala myrtifolia* and *Ochna serrulata.*

## Bowkeria citrina

### Yellow shell-flower bush

**Size:** 2–4 x 1–3 m (wild), up to 3 x 2 m (garden)
**Natural habitat:** This species has a very restricted distribution along the border highlands between KwaZulu-Natal and Mpumalanga. It is found among evergreen scrub along small watercourses.
**Growth form:** It is an erect, multi-stemmed shrub. The leaves have a strong sweet lemon scent when crushed. The flowers are bright yellow and make a wonderful display in early summer. The fruits look as though they are made of polished cardboard, and once they have released the dust-like seed they remain on the tree for some time.
**Propagation:** Seed. Fruits must be collected in autumn just before maturity, and kept in a paper bag to catch the seed. However, it is more practical to take cuttings. New green shoots about 10 cm long are best, and the strike rate is very high in a mist-bed.
**Uses:** Flowering begins at two years and this, coupled with the fragrance of the foliage, makes it a prize item in a small garden. It looks its best next to a water feature. *B. citrina* is fairly slow-growing, about 40 cm per year. It grows well in the garden in areas with temperate summers and a good rainfall. It cannot withstand drought.

## Bowkeria verticillata

### Natal shell-flower bush

**Size:** 2–5 x 2–4 m (wild), up to 3 x 3 m (garden)
**Natural habitat:** *B. verticillata* ranges through the KwaZulu-Natal uplands to the Eastern Cape. It is found on forest edges, particularly among evergreen scrub along small watercourses.
**Growth form:** It is an erect shrub or small tree with dense foliage. The flowers bear a fanciful resemblance to a half-open shellfish. They are white and sticky to the touch, sweetly scented, and glint in the sunshine. They make a good display in late summer. The fruits look as though they are made of polished cardboard, and once they have released the dust-like seed will remain on the tree for some time.
**Propagation:** Seed. Fruits must be collected in autumn just before maturity, and kept in a paper bag to catch the seed. However, it is more practical to take cuttings. New green shoots about 10 cm long are best, and strike well in a mist-bed.
**Uses:** It is pretty enough to be used as a flowering specimen, and its dense foliage mixes well in an informal screen. Growth rate is about 50 cm per year and flowering begins at five years. *B. verticillata* is ideal for a cold garden, growing best in a temperate summer with good rainfall.

**Check your shrub spacing** If you plant your shrubs too closely together you may find that some are smothered and eventually die. Once again, careful planning is the answer. So check each shrub's growth habits and plant them far enough apart.

## Bridelia cathartica

### Knobby bridelia

**Size:** 2–5 x 2–5 m (wild), up to 3 x 3 m (garden)
**Natural habitat:** *B. cathartica* is found in Zululand and in the eastern Lowveld. It grows on forest margins or in bushy scrub.
**Growth form:** It is shrubby in habit, being short and wide-spreading even if single-stemmed, with a tendency to scramble in dense vegetation. *B. cathartica* is more or less evergreen, with a short deciduous period in a dry winter. The glossy leaves have a bluish tinge, and are elegantly veined. The flowers are insignificant, but *B. cathartica* is very attractive when in fruit. The berries are dark mauve, and an important source of food for birds.
**Propagation** Seed, which must be fresh.
**Uses:** In cultivation *B. cathartica* is a useful addition to a bird garden, where it can be used to fringe taller vegetation or be included in a mixed screen. Fruit is produced at an early age, even outside the natural range. *B. cathartica* could be used in a beach garden. It likes a warm summer and high rainfall. The initial growth rate is about 1 m per year under these circumstances, considerably less if rainfall is poor.

## Buddleja auriculata

### Weeping sage

**Size:** 2–4 x 3–5 m (wild), up to 3 x 4 m (garden)
**Natural habitat:** This species of shrub is found naturally in the temperate damp uplands of the east. It occurs at the edges of montane forest and alongside streams.
**Growth form:** *B. auriculata* is always densely shrubby. The branches arch out and down, tending to 'weeping', so that most branch tips touch the ground. The leaves are glossy blackish-green above and white below, the veins forming a richly patterned network. The flowers are small and trumpet-like, and smell of honey. The scent can be detected up to 50 m away. Flowers cover the plant in autumn and early winter. On any one plant the flowers will be the same colour, but on different trees a variety of pastel shades can be seen. They attract butterflies and other nectar-seeking insects.
**Propagation:** Seed or cuttings.
**Uses:** *B. auriculata* is ideal for a wild garden where it is best grown in a mixed bush clump. It is also pretty enough to be used as a foliage and flowering specimen, and makes a good screen. Growth is rapid, at least 1 m per year, and flowering begins usually at two years. *B. auriculata* likes a cool or temperate summer and good rainfall.

**Keep your eyes peeled** Don't rely solely on books to determine exactly how a particular shrub will react to conditions in your garden. Rather look at other gardens in your neighbourhood to see just how various plants respond to the climatic and soil conditions in your area.

## Buddleja dysophylla

**White climbing sage**

**Size:** 3–5 x 2–3 m (wild), up to 4 x 3 m (garden)
**Natural habitat:** This shrub grows naturally in the wetter parts of the southeast, where it occurs in evergreen forests and in damp thickets.
**Growth form:** It is a scrambler that spreads across the ground if there is nothing to climb. The leaves are heart-shaped and pale green with a creamy-white undersurface. The flowers are small and trumpet-like, very similar to those of the exotic species, and smell of honey. Flowering is especially prolific; at a distance the plant appears covered with white mist. Flowering usually takes place in mid-winter, making the display all the more remarkable. The flowers attract butterflies and other nectar-seeking insects.
**Propagation:** Seed or cuttings.
**Uses:** In cultivation *B. dysophylla* is best given a long length of fence as a support, or must be included in a bushy clump. Its lax form also means that it spills elegantly down a steep rocky slope. It grows at least 1 m per year, and flowering begins usually at two years. *B. dysophylla* enjoys a warm or cool climate provided that rainfall is high. It withstands an average winter drought.

## Buddleja glomerata

**Karoo sage**

**Size:** 3–4 x 3–4 m (wild), up to 3 x 3 m (garden)
**Natural habitat:** This well-named species is confined to the Karoo and Eastern Cape. It occurs in scrubby vegetation on rocky slopes and along seasonal stream courses.
**Growth form:** *B. glomerata* is a bushy and upright shrub, occasionally tree-like. It is perhaps the most striking of all the species of *Buddleja*, particularly because of its foliage. The leaves are heavily scalloped, grey-blue when young, maturing to bluish green. The veins are deeply etched and embossed, giving a third dimension to the white undersurface of the leaf; pattern and colour recall a traditional Christmas tree. The flowers are creamy-yellow, and form pyramids all over the plant for extended periods in summer. They smell like honey, and attract butterflies and other nectar-seeking insects.
**Propagation:** Seed or cuttings.
**Uses:** *B. glomerata* makes a good foliage and flowering specimen, and is tidy enough to be used in a conventional garden. It is also ideal for a wild garden where it is best grown in a mixed bush clump. It grows rapidly, at least 1 m per year, and flowering usually begins at two years. It seems to enjoy most climates, and survives extreme heat and drought.

**Attractive greens** Creating a garden is not all about colour and flowers. There are many shades of green and many different leaf shapes. Make full use of these. Contrast dark green glossy with pale grey; fussy shapes with smooth spiky ones. *Buddleja* provides a range of colour, texture and shape.

## Burchellia bubalina

### Wild pomegranate

**Size:** 2–8 x 2–6 m (wild), up to 3 x 4 m (garden)
**Natural habitat:** This species of shrub is found almost throughout the wetter regions, from the southwestern Cape to the eastern Escarpment. It occurs in most evergreen forests, either in the undergrowth or on the fringes, and on rocky outcrops in grassland and scrub.
**Growth form:** It can be a single-stemmed tree, but is nearly always shrubby. *Burchellia* is noted for its flowering display that starts in spring and lasts for several months. The tubular orange flowers are clustered together in small heads. They are visible at a considerable distance and are visited by sunbirds. The fruits do not look appetising but are the favourite of starlings, bulbuls, barbets and even baboons.
**Propagation:** Seed, which should be collected once the fruits have dried and rattle when shaken.
**Uses:** *Burchellia* is ideal for a small garden and deserves prime position. Growth rate is about 30 cm per year. Flowering begins in the second year, and is very reliable subsequently. It also makes a good screen, ideal for mixing with other bird-attracting shrubs. This shrub thrives in most climates except hot dry summers. It enjoys full sunshine, but is equally at home in partial shade, though it flowers less well there.

## Buxus macowanii

### Cape box

**Size:** 3–6 x 3–6 m (wild), up to 3 x 3 m (garden)
**Natural habitat:** *Buxus* has a curious distribution, occurring in the coastal forests of the Eastern Cape, but having an isolated population in the Limpopo Province. This shrub is nearly always found in shady undergrowth.
**Growth form:** Although usually single-stemmed, it branches low down and is densely bushy. The foliage is dense and exquisite, the leaves tiny, dark and very glossy. The flowers are white, and although minute, borne in such abundance in the axil of every leaf, that the shrub appears to be snow-spangled.
**Propagation:** Seed or cuttings.
**Uses:** In cultivation it forms a rounded bush with foliage so neat it almost looks as though it has been clipped. Indeed the European Box, a close relative, has been used as a formal low hedge for well over 2,000 years. *Buxus* grows slowly, at most 30 cm per year. Flowering begins at eight years. Its slow growth makes this shrub particularly suitable for small gardens. It can be used as a specimen or a screen. Although at home in shade it prefers full sun and will only flower well there. It must have a temperate to warm summer with at least moderate rainfall. It tolerates an average winter drought and slight frost.

**Nature's snack bar** Plant shrubs with tubular red flowers to attract sunbirds to your garden. *Burchellia bubalina, Leonotis, Aloe* species and red hot pokers will provide a snack bar for these lovely creatures.

## Cadaba termitaria

**Pink cadaba**

**Size:** 1–4 x 2–6 m (wild), up to 2 x 5 m (garden)
**Natural habitat:** *Cadaba* grows naturally in the hot dry north-east, where it occurs in open woodland. As the name suggests it usually grows on termite mounds, but not exclusively so.
**Growth form:** This shrub is nearly always shrubby, forming a dark mushroom-like mound. The foliage is bluish grey. The delicacy of the flowers is in complete contrast to the otherwise rugged look of *Cadaba*. There are no petals, but a few slender wine-red stamens, capped with yellow anthers, sprout from pale green sepals. The fruits are thin little hanging, grey-green sausages, which peel back from the tip to reveal an orange pulp when they are ripe.
**Propagation:** Seed. It is often dispersed by birds to rural gardens within the natural range.
**Uses:** This shrub is hardly a classical beauty but its frost-hardiness and almost infinite tolerance of drought make it useful in harsh climates. It makes a solid low screen, much used by small birds where other shelter is in short supply. Flowering begins at four years. The foliage colour makes it suitable for a grey theme garden. Growth is slow: a ten-year-old plant has reached 2 m in height and 5 m in diameter.

## Canavalia rosea

**Beach-bean canavalia**

**Size:** 4–10 m long (wild), up to 8 m long (garden)
**Natural habitat:** *Canavalia* is found naturally on the south-east coast. It is one of the first plants found growing on sand dunes just above high-tide level, or grows on forest edges.
**Growth form:** It is a robust scrambler. Plants on forest edges behave as twiners, seeking the canopy. Those growing on dunes are better known, their long new branches creeping across bare sand. They create the hummock dunes of the east coast by binding the sand with their roots; their leaves slow wind and sand movement too. White-fronted sand-plovers nest among debris trapped between the stems. The flowers are reddish purple, pea-like and sweet scented. Carpenter bees and sunbirds visit them. Flowering lasts eight months, from midsummer onwards.
**Propagation:** Seed, which germinates rapidly.
**Uses:** This is a glorious plant for instant results. Allow it to creep over a pergola or fence. The dense foliage casts good shade and is used by birds and lizards as a hiding place. *Canavalia* is exceptionally useful in the most exposed beach gardens where little else will grow. It flowers in its first year, and, in good rains, individual branches can grow 1 m within two weeks. It does not like drought or frost.

**Plant shrubs of varying height** Planting shrubs of a similar height in a straight line can create a rather messy-looking hedge effect. It is preferable to group your shrubs with shorter plants in the front to create an appearance of depth.

## Capparis brassii

### Little caper bush

**Size:** 3–6 m long (wild), up to 4 m long (garden)
**Natural habitat:** This species is restricted to KwaZulu-Natal. It occurs on the fringes of thickets.
**Growth form:** It is a modest, only slightly thorny scrambler, most evident when flowering branches spray out of a bush clump. The leaves are small and glossy. Flowers appear in spring and are striking small sweet-smelling white powder-puffs that attract both insects and sunbirds. They are followed by warty orange fruits. These are very popular with birds, especially starlings, which rip them open as they mature and soften, revealing seeds embedded in red jelly.
**Propagation:** Seed.
**Uses:** *C. brassii* is suitable for a small garden or patio. It is best grown against a small fence or in a bush clump, and is pretty enough to warrant its own place on a trellis. Rate of growth is 1 m or more per year if the summer is warm and rainfall moderate, considerably less in cooler conditions. Flowering begins at about three years if the plant receives full sun: shaded plants flower only if a branch escapes into the sun. Fruiting has yet to be seen outside the natural range.

## Capparis fascicularis

### Wild caper bush

**Size:** 3–8 m long (wild), up to 5 m long (garden)
**Natural habitat:** This species occurs patchily throughout the warmer parts of the east. It is found on the margins of drier forests and in woodland thickets.
**Growth form:** It is a thorny creeper with elegant narrow leaves. Typically it scales a small tree and then its branches drape their way back to the ground. Flowers appear in spring and are most striking, white, sweet-smelling powder-puffs that attract both insects and sunbirds. They are followed by small polished orange fruits that hang in clusters. These are very popular with birds. *C. fascicularis* is the host of many butterflies of the family Pieridae.
**Propagation:** Seed.
**Uses:** *C. fascicularis* is best grown against a fence or in a bush clump. It is also big enough to cover a pergola and is ideal for an informal wildlife garden. Flowering begins at about three years. Fruiting has yet to be seen outside the natural range. Rate of growth is 1 m or more per year if the summer is warm and rainfall moderate, considerably less in cooler conditions.

**'Thornveld'** is the term given to woodland dominated by acacias. 'Lowveld' is woodland found at lower altitudes, especially in Limpopo and Mpumalanga provinces. 'Bush' is a very ambiguous term, which is to be avoided.

## Capparis tomentosa

**Woolly caper bush**

**Size:** 4–10 m long (wild), up to 7 m long (garden)
**Natural habitat:** *C. tomentosa* occurs from the Eastern Cape to the warmer parts of the north and east. It is most common in dense dry woodland.
**Growth form:** This is a vigorous scrambler, with strong curved thorns, enabling it to envelop its support. Typically, branches form a dense tangled mass in the crown of a small tree, finally cascading in a curtain towards the ground. Nesting birds often use *C. tomentosa* tangles. White sweet-smelling powder-puffs, which attract both insects and sunbirds, appear in spring. Fruits are large and orange, and are draped all over the plant. Ripe fruits are very popular with birds, especially starlings, which rip them open, revealing seeds in a red jelly. *C. tomentosa* is the host of many butterflies of the family Pieridae.
**Propagation:** Seed.
**Uses:** *C. tomentosa* is best grown against a fence or in a bush clump, and is ideal for an informal wildlife garden. It will soon cover a 15-m section of fence, or it can be trained over an expendable plant. Flowering begins at about three years. Fruiting has yet to be seen outside the natural range. Rate of growth is 1 m or more per year if the summer is warm and rainfall moderate, much less in cooler conditions.

## Carissa bispinosa

**Num-num**

**Size:** 1–3 m x 1–3 m (wild), up to 2 x 2 m (garden)
**Natural habitat:** It is widespread, extending from the south-western Cape through KwaZulu-Natal and the eastern Free State to the far northeast. It always occurs in dense vegetation and is most common in the undergrowth of mist-belt forest.
**Growth form:** It is an upright spiny shrub, rather sparse when growing in the shade, very dense when in full sun. The leaves are thick and glossy. The spines are borne in neat forked pairs. The flowers are small white stars produced in sweetly scented masses. They are followed by small, long, and thin, edible red fruits enjoyed equally by people and birds.
**Propagation:** Seed or cuttings, and often planted by birds within its natural range.
**Uses:** *C. bispinosa* makes a beautiful garden shrub and eventually a spiny defence if grown as a hedge. First flowering can be expected at two to three years. Growth rate is about 30 cm per year. *C. bispinosa* grows well enough in damp half-shade, but better in full sun, and prolific flowering can be expected only there. It grows best where the summer is warm and the rainfall moderate to good.

**Choose local plants** Choose plants best suited to climatic conditions in your region. Growing unsuitable plants will result in a constant struggle against the prevailing elements, and that is not what gardening should be about. You will enjoy gardening far more if your plants flourish under your local conditions.

## Carissa macrocarpa

Amatungulu

**Size:** 2–5 x 3–6 m (wild), up to 3 x 4 m (garden)
**Natural habitat:** This is a coastal species, growing naturally from Zululand to the Eastern Cape. It occurs in evergreen forest, usually on the margins.
**Growth form:** *C. macrocarpa* is a dense spreading shrub. It is very spiny, the spines being neatly forked. The foliage is brilliant: the leaves thick, leathery and very glossy. Flowers are produced in sweetly scented masses. They are large white stars and make a showy display. The fruits are large, red, softly fleshy and quickly pulled to pieces by birds.
**Propagation:** Seed or cuttings.
**Uses:** *C. macrocarpa* makes a fine specimen and the perfect impenetrable screen. An effective hedge results after three years, in which time flowering and fruiting can be expected. *C. macrocarpa* fruits far outside its natural range, and in a dry climate with extremes of temperature. The fruits can be made into an exquisite jelly. *C. macrocarpa* is especially useful in a sandy coastal garden because it withstands sea winds. It will grow in damp half-shade, though flower poorly there. Growth rate is about 70 cm per year. It grows best where the summer is warm and rainfall moderate to good.

## Carissa tetramera

Sand-forest num-num

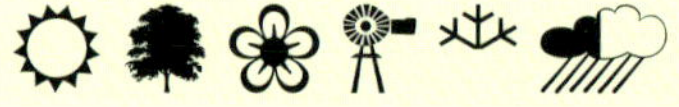

**Size:** 1–3 x 1–2 m (wild), up to 2 x 2 m (garden)
**Natural habitat:** This is found in the Lowveld on sandy soils, either as a low-growing thicket or on the margins of dry forest.
**Growth form:** It is small and erect, the branches spiny. The leaves are small and glossy, new spring growth being bright red. The white flowers are also small, but produced in sweetly scented masses. Unlike other *Carissa* flowers, *C. tetramera* flowers are four-petalled. They appear in spring, and the combination of green and red foliage spangled with white stars, is extremely pretty. Small black berries follow the flowers.
**Propagation:** Seed. *C. tetramera* can also be grown from root cuttings. Pull up a length of root from a wild thicket and cut it into 15-cm lengths. Root cuttings must be laid flat and be completely covered by sand.
**Uses:** It makes a lovely specimen and is especially useful in the tiniest garden. In cold areas it even produces some red autumn leaves, a feature never seen in its normal haunts. Growth rate is about 30 cm per year, but flowering starts in the second year. It grows in all soil types, not just in sand, and tolerates some frost. It grows best where the summer is warm and the rainfall moderate to good.

**Advertising pays** Birds are one of the most important agents for the dispersal of seeds. To attract the birds, bird-dispersed fruits, such as those of *Allophylus*, *Carissa* and *Coccinea*, are usually brightly coloured and highly visible.

## Carissa wyliei

**Forest num-num**

**Size:** 2–4 x 2–3 m (wild), up to 2 x 1 m (garden)
**Natural habitat:** *C. wyliei* is restricted to a few localities in the warmer parts of KwaZulu-Natal and the Eastern Cape. It is found in the forest undergrowth or on the margins.
**Growth form:** It is an erect shrub, with a tendency to scramble, and differs from the other species of *Carissa* in being virtually thornless. The leaves and young branches are a bright, deep, glossy green. The flowers are sweetly scented white stars, a bunch standing erect from almost every shoot. Flowering begins in early spring and is continuous, sometimes profuse, for up to six months. The fruits are red and fleshy.
**Propagation:** Seed or cuttings.
**Uses:** *C. wyliei* makes a good small specimen or component of a low screen. It begins flowering in its second year, making it ideal for the smallest garden. Although growing well enough in partial shade, this shrub revels in full sun, even a hot dry spot or near-neglected pot. Frost tolerance is not known, so in cold areas protect *C. wyliei* by planting it against a north-facing wall. Growth rate is about 30 cm per year. It grows best where the summer is warm and the rainfall moderate to good.

## Cassine papillosa

**Common saffronwood**

**Size:** 2–12 x 2–10 m (wild), up to 3 x 3 m (garden)
**Natural habitat:** *Cassine* occurs in a broad coastal strip extending from the southern Cape to Zululand, and in the mist-belt regions of the KwaZulu-Natal Midlands and the eastern Escarpment. It is confined to forests, usually in shady undergrowth.
**Growth form:** It is nearly always shrubby, although very rarely it becomes a substantial tree. The leaves are its finest feature. They are very stiff and heavily and neatly serrate, almost prickly. The flowers are small and white, but, when massed, make a pleasant display. The fruits are about 2 cm in diameter, pale yellow, spherical, firmly fleshy, and are produced in abundance. Larger fruit-eating birds, such as louries and parrots, enjoy them.
**Propagation:** Seed.
**Uses:** *Cassine* makes an interesting small foliage specimen, usually maintaining a near-spherical shape. It flowers so profusely, when only 50 cm tall, that it makes quite a display, despite the tiny size of the flowers. It enjoys life in full sun, an opportunity denied it in the wild. Growth is slow, about 30 cm per year. It needs a warm summer with at least moderate rainfall, and endures some frost.

**Letting the sunshine in** It is not advisable to plant tall shrubs along the east and north boundaries of your garden, as this will block out the sunlight. It is only the harsh sun from the west that you want to exclude.

## Cassinopsis ilicifolia

**Spiny cassinopsis, Holly cassinopsis**

**Size:** 2–5 x 2–3 m (wild), up to 3 x 3 m (garden)
**Natural habitat:** *Cassinopsis* ranges from the southern Cape through KwaZulu-Natal and the eastern Free State to the northeastern uplands. It conspicuously avoids the warmest part of the country and occurs in evergreen forests and riverine scrub. It looks its best on forest margins.
**Growth form:** It is a scrambling spiny shrub. *Cassinopsis* is evergreen, and adds a new dimension to the term, for even quite thick branches remain green, and only older main trunks lose their chlorophyll. Younger branches have a pleasing zig-zag pattern and the leaves are bright and glossy. *Cassinopsis*'s fruits are small orange plums, snapped up by birds as soon as they mature.
**Propagation:** Seed.
**Uses:** It is a nice foliage specimen and a useful addition to a bird garden in cold areas. If grown without support it develops into a shrub about 2 m tall, subsequent growth going into trailing branches. Trained against a fence, it will span 5 to 8 m. First fruiting occurs at two years. Growth is reasonably fast at about 70 cm per year. *Cassinopsis* likes a temperate or cool summer with moderate to good rainfall. It withstands some drought and fairly heavy frost.

## Catha edulis

**Bushman's tea**

**Size:** 2–5 x 2–5 m (wild), up to 3 x 3 m (garden)
**Natural habitat:** *Catha* ranges from the Eastern Cape, through KwaZulu-Natal to the far northeast. It occurs in a variety of habitats, most often on the rocky banks of seasonal streams.
**Growth form:** In the wild it can be a normal tree, but is so often knocked flat by floods that it is usually a large multi-stemmed bush. The foliage is attractive, the leaves being evenly and perfectly serrate. The flowers are white and small, but borne in massed bunches, almost covering the tree.
**Propagation:** Seed.
**Uses:** In cultivation *Catha* tends to be bushy, and could be used as a screen as well as being elegant enough to make a specimen. Flowering begins at four years. Growth rate is modest, about 30 cm per year. *Catha* likes a warm climate with moderate rainfall. Frost tolerance has not been tested, but *Catha* survives moderate drought. In the Middle East this same plant goes under the name *khat*, and is widely used as a stimulant. It can be chewed or brewed into a tea. Its commercial opportunities have not yet been explored in South Africa.

**Building strong roots** A really good soaking of your garden is far better than frequent sprinkling. The water sinks down into the soil and encourages plants to form deep roots. Surface rooting often results in an unstable plant.

## Catunaregam spinosa

**Thorny bone-apple**

**Size:** 3–6 x 3–5 m (wild), up to 4 x 4 m (garden)
**Natural habitat:** This species is restricted to the warm parts of the east and north. *Catunaregam* occurs most commonly in sand forest, on the margins of other forest types, and in thickets on rocky outcrops.
**Growth form:** It may be tree-like, but is usually multi-stemmed. The branches of young trees form a right-angled pattern and bear fierce spines. Both features are gradually lost with age. *Catunaregam* has pretty, sweetly scented, white flowers in spring. They turn yellow before they fall. The fruits are quite large, yellow and fleshy, reputedly edible, but apparently eaten only by monkeys.
**Propagation:** Seed.
**Uses:** It makes an interesting stand-alone specimen. However, it is best placed in a bush clump, or in a mixed screen where its spines make an effective barrier. Flowering begins at about four years. Although deciduous in the wild, it is rarely so in cultivation. The growth rate is about 50 cm per year. *Catunaregam* enjoys a warm or temperate summer with moderate to good rainfall. This shrub's drought tolerance is moderate; its frost tolerance slight.

## Cephalanthus natalensis

**Tree strawberry**

**Size:** 2–4 x 2–4 m (wild), up to 3 x 3 m (garden)
**Natural habitat:** *Cephalanthus* is found naturally in the uplands of KwaZulu-Natal, and from there to the eastern Escarpment. It occurs in a variety of habitats, notably in dry thornveld, on koppies and on forest edges.
**Growth form:** It may be a small tree, branching low down, or is more usually shrubby. The leaves are small, neat and glossy, and have a pink tinge on the margins and stalks. *Cephalanthus* has unusual and very pretty flowers: they are small red tubes, tipped with white, arranged in spherical heads. The final result is a white pompon with a red under-coat blushing through. The fruit is white and firmly fleshy, with the seeds embedded in its surface in the fashion of a strawberry. It is edible but not exciting.
**Propagation:** Seed, best collected when the fruits have dried on the tree.
**Uses:** *Cephalanthus* is worth growing for its foliage and it is also a good screening plant. First flowering and fruiting are likely at about four years. Growth rate is roughly 60 cm per year. It likes a temperate summer with high to moderate rainfall, but grows well enough in a warm summer if rainfall is good or if it is planted near water.

**Testing for water-logging** If you are worried about water-logging in a section of your garden, check it carefully before planting. Dig a hole 75 x 75 x 75 cm and fill it with water. If it has not drained within an hour, plan a swamp-loving shrub in this area.

## Chrysanthemoides monilifera

**Bush-tick berry**

**Size:** 1–4 x 2–9 m (wild), up to 2 x 5 m (garden)
**Natural habitat:** *Chrysanthemoides* extends from the south-western Cape to the eastern Escarpment, and is found in most habitats from sea level to the top of the Drakensberg. It is often dominant near the beach, enduring seawinds on the exposed face of the first dune.
**Growth form:** *Chrysanthemoides* is usually a vigorous sprawling shrub. Young leaves are covered with a soft fuzz which birds strip off to use as nest lining. Mature leaves have a grey-blue tinge and are glossy with a slight clinging texture when touched. The flowers are bright yellow daisies, present almost throughout the year. The fruits are small and black, sweet-tasting and enjoyed by birds. Many butterflies, notably coppers of the family Lycaenidae, rely on *Chrysanthemoides*.
**Propagation:** Seed.
**Uses:** *Chrysanthemoides* can be used to provide colour and a screen, and is ideal in a bird garden. It is especially useful in windswept beach gardens. Growth rate is initially about 80 cm per year. *Chrysanthemoides* likes moderate to high rainfall and cannot withstand drought. It has yet to be tested in severe frost in an open flat garden. In the mountains it always gets some shelter or the benefit of a slope.

## Clausena anisata

**Perdepis**

**Size:** 2–8 x 2–6 m (wild), up to 4 x 4 m (garden)
**Natural habitat:** *Clausena* occurs in the wetter parts of the south and east. It is common in the interior of evergreen forests and on their margins. It also occurs in bushveld where rocks protect it from fire.
**Growth form:** *Clausena* tends to be shrubby, although can be a neat upright tree. Its leaves are glossy and droop gracefully. A bruised leaf emits a strong smell – not to everyone's taste but with its own unique charm. The gentlest touch produces the scent. The flowers are small white bells, which are followed by small berries that turn from red to black. *Clausena* is host to several spectacular swallowtail butterflies of the genus *Papilio*.
**Propagation:** Seed, which must be fresh.
**Uses:** *Clausena* makes a lovely garden subject. Despite being found most often in the shade in the wild, it prefers full sun in cultivation, flowering after two years, and fruiting heavily at four. It can be used as a specimen in a small garden, or as a fringe for a forest clump. Growth rate is about 80 cm per year initially, slowing as the plant thickens. *Clausena* likes moderate to high rainfall and tolerates moderate frost.

**The view from the sink** If possible, create a lovely view from your kitchen sink. If you have no view into the distance, make sure that you look out onto some special plants, such as *Chrysanthemoides monilifera* and *Grewia flavescens*, with year-round interest. You could, for example, also set up your bird-feeder in this space.

## Clematis brachiata

**Traveller's joy**

**Size:** 4–10 m long (wild), up to 8 m long (garden)
**Natural habitat:** *Clematis* is widespread from sea level to high altitude. This plant appears in most habitats, from fynbos to Karoo, but is most common at forest edges, and especially in thickets and scrub.
**Growth form:** It is a woody climber that holds onto its support with twining leaf stalks. The flowers are white and make a fantastic sweet-scented display in early summer. It can be seen at some distance casting a snowy blanket over its support, with snaky wisps searching for new territory. By autumn the dandelion-like fruits are equally prolific and enchanting. As they mature they are gradually blown away, being carried easily by the lightest breeze.
**Propagation:** Seed or small cuttings.
**Uses:** Of all bigger scramblers *Clematis* is the least dominating. Although it can grow large in a warm climate, it can be easily cut back, to ground level if necessary. In frosty areas this happens naturally, but *Clematis* always recovers in spring, and flowers and fruits within the same year. Support is essential, and *Clematis* grows especially well on a trellis or fence. Growth is rapid, at least 2 m per year. It likes high to moderate rainfall, but tolerates quite extended droughts.

## Cnestis polyphylla

**Itch-pod**

**Size:** 3–7 x 2–4 m (wild), up to 5 x 3 m (garden)
**Natural habitat:** *Cnestis* is found in the warmer parts of the east and southeast. It occurs in forest, most commonly on the edges, and among very thick scrub.
**Growth form:** It is a small shrubby scrambler. Size varies greatly. Without support the plant never exceeds 2 m; with support branches may grow to 5 m. It is a very attractive plant, with long leaves regularly divided into neat leaflets. Mature leaves are distinctly bluish, but towards the branch tips there is an interesting sequence of colour: the newest, outermost leaves are bright red; slightly older leaves are bronze, progressing to very pale green, mid-green, and finally blue-green. The flowers are quite pretty – small white stars borne in sprays. The fruits are red and velvety, splitting to expose a large shiny black-and-yellow seed.
**Propagtion:** Seed, which must be fresh.
**Uses:** This species is best used in a bush clump or against a fence. It takes up little space and the foliage adds to the colour and texture of the garden. Fruiting begins at four years within the natural range, but has not yet been seen outside it. Growth rate is modest, about 1 m per year. *Cnestis* likes a warm, frost-free climate with at least moderate rainfall.

**Pruning tips** Prune shrubs only once they have flowered. Unless practising topiary, choose shrubs whose form and growth habit is best suited to the space in which they will be growing. Constant cutting back to make the plant fit its space will produce awkward, unnatural specimens.

## Coccinea palmata

**Wild cucumber**

**Size:** 3–8 m long (wild), up to 5 m long (garden)
**Natural habitat:** *Coccinea* ranges throughout the east. It occurs on forest edges and in thickets, and is equally at home on the coast and in the Drakensberg.
**Growth form:** It is a modest creeper that climbs using tendrils. The large leaves are striking and maple-shaped. In autumn, as the leaves fall, the hanging fruits demand attention. They are small, smooth cucumbers, which, starting at the tip, progressively blush deep red. Sexes are separate, and only females bear fruit. As the fruits soften over winter, birds eat the lot, then most of the vine disintegrates back to a persistent rootstock. This resprouts in the following spring.
**Propagation:** Seed. This is best planted directly by mashing an over-ripe fruit and spreading the pulp where needed.
**Uses:** Small creepers make good use of vertical space, especially in small gardens. *Coccinea* makes a great screen on a trellis, and softens fences. It is not robust, nor permanent enough for a pergola. It is short-lived – some plants die after a single season – so plant two or three together, and plant more seed each year until the population is self-sustaining. *Coccinea* grows to full size within a single season. Provided rainfall is good it enjoys most climates.

## Coddia rudis

**Small bone-apple**

**Size:** 1–3 x 1–3 m (wild), up to 2 x 2 m (garden)
**Natural habitat:** *Coddia* ranges from the Eastern Cape through KwaZulu-Natal to the eastern Lowveld and Escarpment. It occurs on forest fringes, in bush clumps beneath tall acacias and among rocks.
**Growth form:** It is a dense shrub with unusual arching branches. They grow stiffly upwards, outwards and finally downwards. They tend to be produced in layers so that the overall effect is of a multi-storeyed fountain. The leaves are tiny and branched in small rosettes. *Coddia* is almost evergreen. The flowers are small cream-coloured bells strung along the length of the smaller branches and appear in late spring.
**Propagation:** Seed.
**Uses:** *Coddia* is a most worthwhile shrub and could be grown as a solo specimen. Alternatively, put it on the sunny side of taller vegetation. First flowering occurs at two years. Growth rate is about 40 cm per year. However, the unique growth form develops at an early age and more symmetrically than it does in the wild. *Coddia* thrives in low or high rainfall, provided that the summer is warm. It can also tolerate some frost. *Coddia* makes a good bonsai.

**Rolling frost** Remember that frost rolls downhill so plants at the bottom of the slope will be the worst affected.

## Coffea racemosa

**Wild coffee**

**Size:** 2–5 x 2–4 m (wild), up to 3 x 3 m (garden)
**Natural habitat:** *Coffea* is restricted to the coastal plain in northern Zululand. This shrub occurs in dune forest and other well-wooded habitats.
**Growth form:** It is often shrubby, or may be a small elegant tree with precise horizontal branching. The leaves are neat, wavy and very glossy, the flowers small white stars. After they fall, the yellow calyxes remain, producing an equally attractive show. The fruits are small purple berries, eaten by birds.
**Propagation:** Seed.
**Uses:** *Coffea* makes a delightful small specimen. Flowering begins at two years. A few fruits are produced outside the natural range. Growth rate is about 40 cm per year at the subtropical coast, rather less inland. *Coffea* thrives in all sorts of unlikely conditions. Apart from its value in coastal sand it grows just as well in shale. *Coffea* has been processed commercially to make reasonable coffee, and making your own is simple. Remove the flesh from ripe berries. Ferment the seeds in water for 12 to 24 hours, then dry them for 8 to 10 days, depending on heat and climate. Rub off the outer skins then roast the seeds on a shallow pan to a dark brown colour. Roasting time determines the flavour.

## Combretum bracteosum

**Hiccup nut**

**Size:** 4–8 x 3–5 m (wild), up to 5 x 4 m (garden)
**Natural habitat:** This species occurs in the evergreen forests along the coast of KwaZulu-Natal and the Eastern Cape.
**Growth form:** It is a vigorous scrambler that thrives along forest edges. The flowers are bright red but differ from those of other *Combretum* in that petals are obvious and are responsible for most of the colour. Flowering occurs in spring, flowers being borne towards the tips of branches. The fruits lack wings, the only *Combretum* species in which this is so.
**Propagation:** Seed, which must first be soaked in cold water.
**Uses:** *C. bracteosum* is a fine garden subject, provided enough space is available. It is best grown against a fence or pergola, or in a fringing screen. However, it can also be trained into a striking stand-alone specimen by threading long shoots back into the main body of the plant. Flowering first occurs at two years and is riotous by four years. Growth is very rapid, individual branches growing 2 to 3 m per year. It likes a warm summer with moderate to high rainfall. Frost tolerance is slight; frosted-back plants resprout if damage is not too severe.

**Frost-tender plants** Slightly frost-tender plants can often grow in cold areas if you plant them against a north-facing wall or snugly up against the house. Here the plants will have the benefit of extra protection and warmth.

## Combretum mossambicense

### Knobbly combretum

**Size:** 2–5 x 3–8 m (wild), up to 3 x 5 m (garden)
**Natural habitat:** This is a localised species of the Lowveld, where it occurs in hot dry thickets.
**Growth form:** It is usually shrubby, with a tendency to put out long trailing branches that hang out over thicket edges. *C. mossambicense* is deciduous for several months. It has exceptionally pretty flowers with large white petals surrounding a mass of stamens topped with red anthers. Flowering takes place in spring, when the plant is leafless. The fruits have the usual *Combretum* design, but with five wings. They have the texture and appearance of fine cardboard.
**Propagation:** Seed, which must be fresh and free of parasites. When collecting fruit, check for viability by pulling opposite wings apart. If the fruit is empty, or contains a contented grub, discard it. Probably most of the fruit on the same plant will be in a similar condition.
**Uses:** This shrub's rather untidy growth habit makes it unsuited for use as a conventional specimen. It is better planted against a fence where trailing branches can be accommodated. Growth rate is about 1 m per year, and flowering begins at two years. Fruiting occurs far outside the natural range. It enjoys heat and moderate to low rainfall.

## Combretum paniculatum

### Burning bush, Flame creeper

**Size:** 10–25 m long (wild), up to 14 m long (garden)
**Natural habitat:** This species is found naturally in Zululand and the eastern Lowveld. It occurs on the fringes of riverine forest and on steep bushy slopes alongside streams.
**Growth form:** It is a vigorous scrambler that grows over the tops of thickets and canopies of large riverine trees. Its flowers are outstanding bright red brushes, closely massed along the whole length of the branches, usually before spring leaves have emerged. The whole plant appears red for several weeks. The fruits have the texture and appearance of fine cardboard, cut and shaped to form miniature four-winged mobiles. They are a pretty pale pink, maturing to dull yellow.
**Propagation:** Seed, which must be fresh and free of parasites.
**Uses:** *C. paniculatum* needs space. It must be grown against a fence or pergola, or allowed to tumble down a steep north-facing bank. Growth is very rapid, individual branches elongating 2 to 4 m per year; a single plant can cover 20 m of fencing within three years. First flowering occurs at two years, and is riotous by four. *C. paniculatum* likes a warm summer with moderate to low rainfall. It tolerates mild frost.

**Planning ahead** Before planting a shrubbery, commit your rough plan to paper and draw circles showing the eventual size of each plant. This will give you a good idea of how far apart to plant your shrubs.

## Cordia monoica

### Snot berry

**Size:** 2–4 x 2–4 m (wild), up to 3 x 4 m (garden)
**Natural habitat:** *Cordia* is restricted to the Lowveld and Zululand. It occurs in deciduous woodland.
**Growth form:** It is nearly always a multi-stemmed shrub with stiff branches that arch outwards and downwards. The bark is striking and unusual. It is a variety of shades of very pale brown and grey, giving it a 'peeled' appearance reminiscent of a guava trunk. The leaves have the texture of sandpaper. *Cordia* produces an abundant and showy crop of fruit in summer. The bright orange fruits are fleshy and very sticky, and extremely popular with birds.
**Propagation:** Seed.
**Uses:** *Cordia* is not a classic horticultural beauty, but is worth growing for its branching pattern, bark and fruits. A nice specimen results after five years. First fruiting occurs at two years, prolifically and outside the natural range. The leaves are rough enough to be used as an abrasive to rub down wood. *Cordia* likes a warm climate with moderate to low rainfall. This shrub's growth is rapid, about 1 m per year in a warm climate. It is probably frost-sensitive.

## Crotalaria capensis

### Cape rattle-pod

**Size:** 2–4 x 2–4 m (wild), up to 3 x 3 m (garden)
**Natural habitat:** *Crotalaria* is widespread in the wetter parts of South Africa, ranging from the southwestern Cape to the northeastern Escarpment. It is common on the margins of evergreen forests and alongside streams.
**Growth form:** It tends to be shrubby, but may be a miniature upright tree. The foliage is rather sparse, although the leaves, each divided into three leaflets, are quite attractive. Young growth is silvery blue. *Crotalaria* has very pretty flowers. These are yellow, sometimes tinged red, pea-shaped and produced in abundance in summer. The fruit is a small tubular hollow pod that rattles once the seeds are dry. *Crotalaria* is host to several small blue butterflies of the family Lycaenidae.
**Propagation:** Seed.
**Uses:** *Crotalaria* is ideal for a small garden. It can be used as a specimen flowering shrub, or mixed in an informal bed or screen. Flowering first occurs in the second year, and is regular and profuse thereafter. Growth is rapid – about 1 m per year initially. *Crotalaria* enjoys most temperatures but must have moderate to good rainfall. Drought tolerance is poor.

**Safe in the garden** Many plants, such as *Carissa bispinosa*, *Clausena anisata* and *Strophanthus speciosus*, are often found deep in the shade of natural forests. But, they only grow there because the forest protects them from grass fires. They actually grow better in sunshine, if protected from fire, and will thrive in the safety of your garden.

## Croton menyhartii

### Rough-leaved croton

**Size:** 1–3 x 1–2 m (wild), up to 2 x 2 m (garden)
**Natural habitat:** *C. menyhartii* is found naturally in the eastern Lowveld where it tends to form thickets fringing bush clumps or dry forest on sandy soils.
**Growth form:** It is delicately shrubby. The foliage is most attractive. The leaves are typically *Croton* – silvery-white beneath. *C. menyhartii* continuously sheds leaves a few at a time. Ageing leaves turn a beautiful yellow-orange and remain on the tree for several weeks so that the green and silver is always flecked with orange. The flowers are small white pompons and have modest charm. The shrub's fruits are attractive three-lobed pale speckled capsules.
**Propagation:** Seed.
**Uses:** *C. menyhartii* makes an interesting foliage specimen. It makes a useful filler for a sunny dry corner. Excess water inhibits the formation of orange leaves. It grows well in shale, despite being confined to sand in the wild. Initial growth rate is about 50 cm per year. Moderate to high rainfall is desirable. Frost tolerance is unlikely.

## Croton pseudopulchellus

### Small lavender croton

**Size:** 1–4 x 1–4 m (wild), up to 2 x 3 m (garden)
**Natural habitat:** *C. pseudopulchellus* is found in Zululand and the warmer parts of the north. It occurs in dry forests in partial shade.
**Growth form:** It may be a small tree, but is nearly always shrubby. The leaves are exquisite, typically *Croton* – silvery-white beneath with scattered rusty spots creating a pepper-and-salt effect. Ageing leaves turn a beautiful orange and remain on the tree for several weeks so that the green and silver is always flecked with orange. The combination of intensity of colour and delicacy of texture is without parallel. Butterflies always attend the flowers – small white pompons.
**Propagation:** Seed.
**Uses:** The prettiest of all shrubs, this is a must for a tiny garden. It can be grown in a flowerbed, a shrubbery or as a specimen. Flowering begins at three years and the glorious technicoloured foliage is maintained all year. It attains maximum height and spread within three or so years, thickening subsequently. It grows much better in full sun, and a warm climate with at least moderate rainfall is desirable. Protect from light frost against a north-facing wall.

**Making the most of spring and autumn** Avoid using only evergreen shrubs in your garden. The autumnal colours of deciduous plants are beautiful, and spring foliage brings a special wonder to the garden. *Croton menyhartii* has lovely autumn colours, and *Eugenia* has spring flushes.

## Croton steenkampianus

**Marsh croton**

**Size:** 1–3 x 1–2 m (wild), up to 3 x 2 m (garden)
**Natural habitat:** This species occurs only in northern Zululand where it is found in sand forest, either in complete shade or in half-shade on the fringes. Despite its common name it does not grow well in waterlogged soil.
**Growth form:** It is a small spindly shrub. Epiphytic orchids grow well on its bark. The leaves are very attractive, quite large and soft, pale green above, snow-white below. Any breeze will agitate the leaves so that the white undersurfaces flash. The flowers are small white pompons and have modest charm. The fruits are attractive three-lobed capsules.
**Propagation:** Seed.
**Uses:** This species makes a pretty addition to a shrubbery in a warm garden, however small. It can be used to form a miniature avenue along a secluded path. Once the plants mature, their white leaf undersurfaces dominate, converting the avenue into a silver-lined archway. In a high-rainfall area *C. steenkampianus* thrives in full sun or in partial shade. In drier areas it prefers some shade, although will not flower there.

## Cryptocarya wyliei

**Red-haired laurel**

**Size:** 2–4 x 2–4 m (wild), up to 3 x 2 m (garden)
**Natural habitat:** This is endemic to the Pondoland sandstone outcropping on the KwaZulu-Natal coast. It grows in forest, usually on the margins or on rocky outcrops.
**Growth form:** It is nearly always small and shrubby. The foliage is most attractive. The leaves are small and bicoloured, green above, pale blue with rusty veins below. The fruits are large and bright orange, and make a fine spectacle. They are delicious to eat and are attractive to birds.
**Propagation:** Seed.
**Uses:** *Cryptocarya* is an exquisite shrub in cultivation, given high rainfall, warm summers and frost-free winters. Under these circumstances, and if grown in full sun, it performs better in a garden than it does in the wild, where it has to evade fire, and is virtually condemned to the shade. First fruiting occurs at three years, even outside the natural range. In a small garden *Cryptocarya* demands pride of place. Growth rate is about 40 cm per year in sun. Under poor conditions growth is much slower, and fruiting will be reduced or even suppressed. Frost will probably prove fatal.

**'Potting on'** Plants need to be 'potted on' into bigger pots as they grow, but don't put a small plant straight into the large pot it will eventually need, as the soil could become sour and unhealthy. Potting on in stages enables fresh growing medium to be added when most needed.

## Cussonia zuluensis

### Zulu cabbage tree

**Size:** 2–4 x 1–2 m (wild), up to 3 x 2 m (garden)
**Natural habitat:** *C. zuluensis* occurs in most warm areas in northern and eastern KwaZulu-Natal. It grows in evergreen forest, but more often in thick dry scrub or bush clumps.
**Growth form:** It has an unusual shape. Usually two, three or four spindly, parallel stems rise from the base or from a very low fork. The plant often appears top-heavy. The leaves are huge, the stalk alone being half a metre long. The leaves are divided into leaflets, themselves dissected and serrated in a complex pattern. The flowers are small and greenish, but borne in long spikes, resembling the arms of a candelabra. The fruits are dull red to black, juicy and loved by birds. *C. zuluensis* fruits heavily, and fruiting branches often sag onto the surrounding bush.
**Propagation:** Seed. Seedlings will grow best if they are planted out when still small.
**Uses:** This shrub's unusual form adds a new texture to garden structure. *C. zuluensis* takes up very little space, yet has great impact. It is also ideal as part of a bush clump in a bird garden. Growth rate is about 80 cm per year. It likes high rainfall and is frost-sensitive. However, it can be sheltered from frost adjacent to sunny north-facing walls.

## Dalbergia armata

### Hluhluwe vine, Thorny rope

**Size:** 10–30 m long (wild), up to 15 m long (garden)
**Natural habitat:** This species of shrub grows naturally from the Eastern Cape to the warmer regions east and north. It usually occurs in evergreen forest.
**Growth form:** *D. armata* is a rampant climber capable of scaling the tallest tree. The trunk develops spines as climbing aids at an early age, and these continue to grow throughout the plant's life. Mature trunks bear spectacular and ferocious masses of spines up to 10 cm long. The leaves are delicate and pale, and spill in graceful cascades from the forest canopy. The small white flowers are borne in large sweet-smelling bunches that attract insects.
**Propagation:** Seed or cuttings.
**Uses:** This is not a conventional garden plant, nor does its sparse foliage provide a complete screen. Nevertheless the formidable spines make a good barrier and have a bizarre beauty of their own. *D. armata* grows at least 2 m per year once established, provided that a fence or pergola is available for support. Flowering begins at about three years. *D. armata* likes a warm summer with moderate to good rainfall. When heavily pruned in a small pot, *D. armata* forgets its climbing habits and becomes a lovely bonsai.

**Bold trio** For an interesting focal point try planting three *Cussonia zuluensis* in the same hole. Let them grow naturally – they will make a bold statement.

## Dalbergia nitidula

### Glossy flat-bean

**Size:** 2–5 x 3–6 m (wild), up to 3 x 5 m (garden)
**Natural habitat:** This is a species of the warm north and east, where it is found in deciduous woodland.
**Growth form:** It is nearly always shrubby, wider than tall, typically with most branches radiating from a very short trunk. There may be a short deciduous period. *D. nitidula* has the finest flowering display of any indigenous shrub. The flowers are white and pea-shaped, and borne in masses along every lateral branch. Much of the beauty of the display is due to the fact that all the flowers mature simultaneously. The effect is complemented by an exquisite scent, sweet with a citrus tang. The fruits are small papery pods.
**Propagation:** Seed or cuttings.
**Uses:** *D. nitidula* is a wonderful flowering specimen; ideal for any garden where there is a suitable climate – warm summer with moderate to good rainfall. First flowering occurs at four years. *Dalbergia* flowers have the added distinction of being among the oldest of all known flowers; their fossils have been found in Cretaceous rocks 92 million years old. Growth is fairly quick, maximum size being attained after eight years. Frost tolerance is probably nil.

## Dalbergia obovata

### Climbing flat-bean

**Size:** 3–10 x 2–5 m (wild), up to 6 x 3 m (garden)
**Natural habitat:** *D. obovata* is found naturally in a broad coastal strip extending from the Eastern Cape to Zululand. It occurs in a variety of wooded habitats ranging from evergreen forest margins to dry deciduous woodland.
**Growth form:** Initially shrubby, it puts out long branches bearing helix-shaped hooks that cling to the surrounding vegetation. The leaves have fairly large dark glossy leaflets borne in a slight zig-zag, and are very handsome. *D. obovata* may be briefly deciduous. The flowers are pretty, small and white, but borne in large sweet-smelling bunches which attract lots of insects. The fruits are small pods, with one or two seeds visible through the walls.
**Propagation:** Seed or cuttings.
**Uses:** *D. obovata* has fairly dense foliage, and so makes an adequate screen that spans about 8 m when grown along a fence. It could also be part of a bush clump or mixed screen. Flowering begins at about three years. The characteristic helixes develop in the second year provided that contact is made with a nearby support. Growth is quick: at least 1 m per year. This species thrives in most climates, wet or dry, warm or temperate. It withstands some frost.

**Using liquid fertiliser on potplants** It is very important to wet the soil in pots before applying any fertiliser. If you put liquid fertiliser onto dry soil, its concentration will be too high, and you will burn your precious plant.

## Dermatobotrys saundersii

### Dermatobotrys

**Size:** 1 x 1 m (wild), 1 x 1 m (garden)
**Natural habitat:** This has a restricted range, being confined to the forests of the south-eastern coast and parts of the KwaZulu-Natal interior.
**Growth form:** *Dermatobotrys* is an epiphytic shrub, always lodged in a large tree-fork. It is not a parasite, but roots in leaf litter that collects between branch forks. The leaves are almost succulent, green with a purple tinge. The red pigment serves as a reflective layer to 'recycle' light passing through the leaf by bouncing it back up again. The flowers are glorious deep red trumpets, followed by sweet edible fig-like fruits.
**Propagation:** Seed or cuttings.
**Uses:** *Dermatobotrys* cannot be treated like a conventional shrub. It makes a great pot plant, but avoid contact with soil; it is prone to eelworm if its container is merely put on the ground. Treat it as an epiphyte, suspending it in a well-drained hanging basket, using just leaf litter or compost as the growing medium. Withhold water in winter to get best flowering. *Dermatobotrys* flowers best in full sun, but develops the most richly coloured leaves in shade. Growth is quick, full size and flowering coinciding at two years. A warm climate with good summer rainfall is essential.

## Diospyros austro-africana

### Fire-sticks, Kersbos

**Size:** 1–4 x 1–4 m (wild), up to 3 x 3 m (garden)
**Natural habitat:** This species is found naturally in the cool uplands of KwaZulu-Natal, the central Highveld, extending through parts of the Karoo to the Western Cape mountains. It is most common alongside streams, provided that large trees are absent, or may occur among rocks.
**Propagation:** Seed.
**Growth form:** It is usually a dense, rounded, more or less evergreen shrub. The leaves are small and bluish-grey, turning deep red, almost black, in a hard frost. The flowers are small and pale red, and can be quite attractive. Fruits are borne only on female trees. They are fleshy and red or black, but for most of their career are clasped by velvety reddish brown calyxes. Birds enjoy the fruits.
**Uses:** *D. austro-africana* makes a neat bush, its grey foliage contrasting with other garden colours. First flowering occurs at about four years. It is fairly slow-growing in cultivation, gaining about 40 cm per year. This shrub grows best where the summer is temperate or cool and the rainfall moderate to high, but will survive almost any adversity. It is especially useful at higher altitudes and in areas where severe frost kills nearly everything else.

**Fire treatment for hard seeds** Give large, hard seeds that aren't germinating 'fire treatment' to aid the germination process. Pile dry grass over a heap of seeds and set it alight. There are bound to be seeds that get the optimum scorch, wherever they happen to be in the seed pile.

## Diospyros lycioides

**Bloubos**

**Size:** 2–5 x 2–4 m (wild), up to 3 x 3 m (garden)
**Natural habitat:** *D. lycioides* is very widespread, being absent only from the Western Cape and central Karoo. It occurs in most habitats except the interior of evergreen forest, and is very common in dry woodland and in the highlands.
**Growth form:** It tends to be an upright shrub, but may make a neat small tree. The foliage is distinctly bluish, and in some areas turns a rich red in autumn. The flowers are small creamy bells that line up along the branches. The fruits are red and resemble miniature apples. They make lovely massed displays in late autumn. In the centre of the fruit a delicious jelly encloses a few large pips. Only female plants bear fruits. Birds enjoy them.
**Propagation:** Seed.
**Uses:** *D. lycioides* is not a conventional garden beauty but has rugged charm. It is a particularly good bird plant, so include it in a bird garden. It is also ideal for an informal screen or bush clump. It grows about 60 cm per year, and flowers at three years. *D. lycioides* thrives in any climate, wet or dry, hot or cold. It survives virtually any drought, frost and neglect, so can be used in the most desolate places.

## Diospyros rotundifolia

**Dune jackal-berry**

**Size:** 3–6 x 3–6 m (wild), up to 4 x 4 m (garden)
**Natural habitat:** In South Africa this shrub is confined to a very narrow coastal strip from St Lucia northwards. It occurs in dune forest and is common on the seaward face of the first dune.
**Growth form:** *D. rotundifolia* may be shrubby or treelike, but is always stiffly upright. The disciplined effect is enhanced by the upswept round leathery leaves. The flowers are small white trumpets and can be pretty. The fruits are just like miniature glossy deep red apples, and can make a spectacular display. Inside the fruit an edible jelly encloses a few large pips. Only female plants bear fruits. Birds enjoy them.
**Propagation:** Seed.
**Uses:** When grown in full sun, *D. rotundifolia* is multi-stemmed and makes a good screen. If there is partial shade it makes a small narrow tree. It is densely evergreen under all conditions. Growth rate is about 40 cm per year, with fruit first appearing – at the coast, although well south of the natural range – at ten years. *D. rotundifolia* is most useful in beach gardens, but grows very well inland. It is not dependent upon sand, and enjoys shale, withstanding slight frost.

**Woodland** This habitat is much sparser than forest, and there is plenty of light at ground level. Grass can grow in this environment, so the danger of fire is always present. Shrubs from this habitat are usually deciduous and drought resistant; *Diospyros lycioides* and *Pavetta gardeniifolia* are good examples.

## Diospyros simii

### Star-apple

**Size:** 2–4 x 2–3 m (wild), up to 3 x 3 m (garden)
**Natural habitat:** This species has a fairly restricted range, occupying a broad coastal strip from the Eastern Cape to Zululand. It is usually found on the edges of forests or thickets.
**Growth form:** It may be a tree with drooping branches, but is an opportunistic scrambler, its backward-directed branches being an adaptation for this career. Some stems bear mainly small leafless reversed branchlets, and operate like grappling irons. The small white flowers make a brief pleasing display. *D. simii* can be spectacular when adorned with bunches of bright red fruits. They are borne only on female trees. They resemble miniature apples. Inside the fruit is an edible jelly and a few large pips. Birds enjoy the fruits.
**Propagation:** Seed.
**Uses:** In cultivation, *D. simii* will grow as an untidy shrub, but performs better if given a fence or thorny bush clump to lounge over. It fruits outside its natural range. Initial growth rate is about 50 cm per year and once supported, individual branches may grow quickly to 6 m in length, though the plant never gets too rampant. *D. simii* likes a warm summer, is reasonably drought-hardy and has yet to be tested in frost.

## Diospyros villosa

### Hairy star-apple

**Size:** 1–3 x 1–2 m (wild), up to 2 x 2 m (garden)
**Natural habitat:** This species occurs from the Eastern Cape to warmer parts north and east, where it is found in damp forested areas. It nearly always occurs on forest margins.
**Growth form:** It is a rambling shrub noted for its foliage. The leaves have a three-dimensional texture, created by the countersunk red veins. The petioles are also red. The impact of the leaves is magnified by their arrangement, groups being borne all in a single plane. The small cream flowers put on a brief display. The fruits, which are borne only on female trees, give rise to the common name of star-apple. They are fleshy but firm and for most of their development are enclosed by a furry 'star' formed by the calyx.
**Propagation:** Seed.
**Uses:** In cultivation, *D. villosa* can be treated as a shrub, although it is a bit straggly. It grows quickly to its maximum size. It is best planted against a fence or on the edge of a bush clump, and is ideal for a mixed small screen. With a little support it puts out longer branches that spill out into the sunshine. *D. villosa* likes warm conditions with moderate to good rainfall.

**At the nursery** The tallest plant at the nursery is not always the best one. Choose a shrub with a well-formed growing point (this is the leading shoot that grows upwards), a thick stem, and healthy, blemish-free foliage. The biggest specimen might be pot-bound and struggle to get going once planted out.

## Diospyros whyteana

### Bladder-nut

**Size:** 2–8 x 2–6 m (wild), up to 3 x 3 m (garden)
**Natural habitat:** *D. whyteana* is widespread, being absent only from the northern Lowveld and the arid west. It is common in the undergrowth of montane, mist-belt and coastal forests, or may dominate scrub among rocks on hillsides.
**Growth form:** It may be a small neat tree, but is usually small and shrubby. *D. whyteana* has exquisite leaves; small, very dark and brilliantly glossy. The flowers are small white hanging bells and appear in early spring. The fruits are borne only on female trees. They are loosely wrapped in papery balloons, like those of the Cape gooseberry. At first pale green, the outer casing blushes red, at which stage it gets ripped open by birds seeking the soft inner fruit.
**Propagation:** Seed.
**Uses:** *D. whyteana* is one of the most attractive garden shrubs, the foliage retaining its beauty throughout the year. It deserves a prime spot as a specimen, or a place on the sunny fringe of an evergreen forest patch. It tolerates partial shade. Growth rate is about 50 cm per year. *D. whyteana* likes moderate to high rainfall and is equally at home in a cool or warm summer. It grows particularly well in the southwestern Cape. *D. whyteana* makes a fine bonsai.

## Dodonaea angustifolia

### Sand olive

**Size:** 2–7 x 2–6 m (wild), up to 4 x 4 m (garden)
**Natural habitat:** *Dodonaea* ranges from the southwestern Cape to the KwaZulu-Natal coastal plain. It is found in almost every habitat except the interior of evergreen forests.
**Growth form:** It can be a thickset tree, but tends to be shrubby and upswept. The glossy leaves are long and narrow. *Dodonaea* is more or less evergreen, but in a dry autumn a few leaves turn purple and the foliage thins. The flowers are short-lived and unexceptional, but the fruits are pretty. They bear papery straw-yellow or pinkish wings and persist in masses on the tree for many weeks.
**Propagation:** Seed.
**Uses:** In cultivation most of the lower branches are retained, making *Dodonaea* ideal for a fast-growing screen. Seedlings planted 3 m apart will close up within three years. Growth is fast, about 1 m per year, and fruiting begins in the second year. *Dodonaea* is especially useful because of its tolerance of a wide range of environmental conditions. It grows equally well in shale or deep sand, and, because it resists coastal winds, it can be used to stabilise sand dunes. It likes moderate to high rainfall, but survives considerable drought. It thrives in all temperatures, including fairly heavy frost.

**Be wary of weeding** Weeding can be overdone, as bare soil invites more weeds. In a wildlife garden, where tidiness is not a consideration, allow unknown seedlings to identify themselves. This may be the only way to avoid uprooting desirable plants that have sprouted from seeds blown into the garden or deposited by birds.

## Dombeya burgessiae

**Pink dombeya**

**Size:** 2–5 x 3–6 m (wild), up to 3 x 4 m (garden)
**Natural habitat:** This shrub is found naturally in the warmer parts of the east. It occurs in a variety of bushy habitats.
**Growth form:** It is a chunky shrub, which retains all its branches at ground level. The leaves are large and shaped in the style of a maple. The flowers may cover the plant, and are exceptionally fine, large by *Dombeya* standards, and vary in colour from pale to deep pink. Flowering commences from midsummer onwards, lasting well into autumn. *D. burgessiae* is often full of white-eyes looking for insects.
**Propagation:** Seed, which must be collected as soon as the flower has dried out, before the central capsule splits.
**Uses:** *D. burgessiae* is widely cultivated. It never becomes excessively large, so makes the ideal flowering specimen in almost every garden. This shrub also makes a good screen, and rapidly fills out to hide an ugly corner. First flowering occurs at about three years. Growth rate is about 1 m per year. Best performance results where rainfall is moderate to high, and the summer warm. It survives moderate frost, rapidly recovering if cut back by the winter cold. Indeed, in the absence of frost it flowers better if cut back anyway.

## Dombeya pulchra

**Silver dombeya**

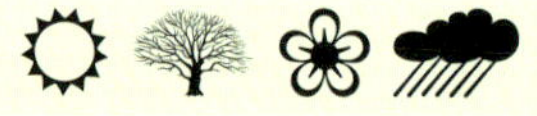

**Size:** 3–5 x 2–4 m (wild), up to 4 x 3 m (garden)
**Natural habitat:** This is endemic to the northeastern Drakensberg. It occurs along wooded watercourses.
**Growth form:** *D. pulchra* branches at ground level, but all branches sweep up, so the plant is always taller than it is wide. The leaves are huge and maple-like, with a texture of dense velvet and give the shrub a lush appearance. Its leafless period is short. The flowers are glorious, cup-shaped, very pale pink with a deep pink centre, and may dominate the plant in midsummer.
**Propagation:** Seed, which must be collected as soon as the flower has dried out, before the central capsule splits.
**Uses:** Most foliage is retained near ground level, so this shrub makes a good, instant screen as well as a lovely foliage and flower plant. *D. pulchra* never becomes excessively large, so makes an ideal flowering specimen in almost every garden. First flowering occurs at about three years. Growth is very fast, at least 1 m per year. It likes a warm summer with at least moderate rainfall. It has yet to be tested in drought or frost.

**Handle cuttings with care** Cuttings are delicate. Do not push them into the growing medium and so damage the cut surface. Make a custom-built hole for them first.

## Dovyalis caffra

### Kei-apple

**Size:** 3–8 x 3–6 m (wild), up to 4 x 4 m (garden)

**Natural habitat:** This species of shrub is common in the warmer parts of the east and north. It is found in many habitats, including evergreen coastal forest clumps and dry woodland, often on termite mounds.

**Growth form:** Young plants have markedly stiff branches that curve up, outwards and finally downwards. They bear extremely thick and strong spines, rendering the plants virtually impregnable. Older plants have fewer spines. Masses of small sweet-scented flowers cover the twigs in August, to be followed by yellow-orange plum-like fruits in midsummer. They have a sharp refreshing flavour, and few escape the attention of the birds.

**Propagation:** Seed, which must be fresh.

**Uses:** The fruit of *Dovyalis* makes an exquisite jam. First fruiting occurs at about three years. It is best to plant at least three plants initially as sexes are separate and only females bear fruit. *Dovyalis* tends to retain its lower branches and so creates a lovely hedge, although it may be partially deciduous in a marginal climate. It is also ideal in a bush clump in a bird garden. Growth rate is about 60 cm per year. *Dovyalis* likes a warm summer with moderate rainfall.

## Dracaena aletriformis

### Large-leaved dragon tree

**Size:** 1–3 x 1 m (wild), up to 2 x 1 m (garden)

**Natural habitat:** *Dracaena* extends from the Eastern Cape to the warmer parts of the east and north. Common in dune and coastal lowland forests, it may dominate the undergrowth.

**Growth form:** This shrub is related to the exotic agaves and sisal. It is a small soft-wooded plant with a very tropical appearance. It is sometimes single-stemmed, but tends to fork once or twice, producing a slender shrub. The leaves are narrow and very large. Flowering displays are spectacular. The flowers are white and borne in massive bunches. They open at night and exude a strong sweet smell. The sticky orange fruits are produced in large clusters and are eaten by birds. The butterfly *Artitropa erinnys* breeds on *Dracaena*.

**Propagation:** Seed.

**Uses:** *Dracaena* makes a beautiful form, foliage, flowering and fruiting specimen. It is suitable for the tiniest space, for example in a pot on a patio, and even indoors. It likes partial shade as well as full sun, and makes a luxuriant thicket beneath a large tree with an open canopy. It makes the perfect filler in a tropical bird garden. Growth rate is about 60 cm per year. Flowering begins at three years. It enjoys a warm summer and good rainfall.

**Swamp forest** This type of forest is always found in low-lying areas and contains a few water-logged soil specialists such as *Kraussia floribunda* and *Tarenna pavettoides*, and a few ordinary lowland species like *Dracaena aletriformis*.

## Duvernoia aconitiflora

**Small pistol bush**

**Size:** 2–4 x 2–4 m (wild), up to 3 x 4 m (garden)
**Natural habitat:** This shrub has a very restricted distribution. *D. aconitiflora* is found in riverine growth on the banks of the Komati River south of Komatipoort.
**Growth form:** It is always shrubby but erect. The flowers are white and very beautiful. At first glance they resemble orchids. The flowering period lasts two to three months, and individual flowers stay in their prime for up to two weeks. They are followed by entertaining fruits which resemble small green clubs. They mature over winter, turning brown and splitting explosively in spring, scattering the seeds. The explosions are reminiscent of a popular breakfast cereal rather than a pistol, and on a warm dry afternoon the plant crackles at regular intervals.
**Propagation:** Seed or cuttings. To harvest seed, you must pick the fruit as it turns brown and keep it in a cloth bag until it splits.
**Uses:** *D. aconitiflora* makes a lovely flowering specimen; one-year-old plants flower, even when still potted. Branches are retained at ground level, making this plant a perfect screen. It needs a warm summer with at least moderate rainfall. Growth rate is at least 60 cm per year. Frost tolerance is unknown, though it tolerates some drought.

## Duvernoia adhatodoides

**Pistol bush**

**Size:** 3–8 x 3–7 m (wild), up to 5 x 4 m (garden)
**Natural habitat:** This species is confined to KwaZulu-Natal and the Eastern Cape where it occurs in warm evergreen forests, usually at the edges.
**Growth form:** It tends to be shrubby, although erect and vigorous. It has large, languid leaves with a tropical look. At first glance the flowers resemble orchids. They are white, streaked inside with purple. They develop in autumn and may cover the tree. Flowering lasts two to three months and individual flowers stay in their prime for up to two weeks. The smell is sweet but slightly sickly. The fruits resemble small green clubs. These turn brown over winter, splitting explosively, scattering the seeds in spring. On a dry, warm afternoon the plant crackles regularly, and the flat seeds can be heard in flight. Black-and-orange carpenter bees frequent this shrub.
**Propagation:** Seed or cuttings. To harvest seed, you must pick the fruit as it turns brown and keep it in a cloth bag until it splits.
**Uses:** *D. adhatodoides* makes a fine specimen and a dense screen. Growth is rapid – more than a metre per year. First flowering occurs at two years. It tolerates some shade, but flowers less well there. It needs a warm summer with at least moderate rainfall. Frost tolerance is unknown.

**Protecting your garden from wind** If you live in an area where a cold wind prevails, get your hardy windbreaking plants established first, as protection for the rest of your garden. Only when they are growing well should you begin to grow other plants. By doing this, you will save yourself a lot of heartbreak and money.

## Ehretia amoena

### Sandpaper bush

**Size:** 2–4 m x 2–4 m (wild), up to 3 x 3 m (garden)
**Natural habitat:** *E. amoena* is restricted to the warmer parts of the east, where it is found in dense, dry woodland.
**Growth form:** It can be a small tree but tends to be shrubby. The branches are usually arched outwards and downwards, but they sometimes grow in every direction. The foliage is sparse and undistinguished but the white flowers are pretty and make a nice display in spring. They are followed by lavish crops of orange, sweet-tasting berries, which are always very popular with birds.
**Propagation:** Seed.
**Uses:** *E. amoena* has an unusual shape and is rarely described as a horticultural beauty, yet has many qualities that recommend it. Its value to birds makes it ideal in a bird garden, where it is best planted in a mixed bush clump. Flowering begins in the fourth year. Growth rate is about 50 cm per year. It grows well in a warm summer with moderate rainfall, but tolerates high rainfall where drainage is good. Frost tolerance is unknown; drought tolerance is moderate.

## Ehretia rigida

### Deurmekaarbos

**Size:** 2–6 x 2–6 m (wild), up to 4 x 4 m (garden)
**Natural habitat:** This shrub is found almost everywhere in South Africa and is often sown by birds in gardens in drier areas. It occurs in most habitats, except the interior of evergreen forests, and is especially common in thick dry woodland.
**Growth form:** *Ehretia* can be a small tree but tends to be shrubby. The branches usually curve stiffly upwards, outwards and finally downwards, sometimes even touching the ground, though sometimes they grow in every direction. The leaves are usually borne in neat bunches. The flowers are a pretty pale-mauve and make a nice display in spring. These are followed by heavy crops of red, sweet-tasting berries that are a great favourite with birds and people.
**Propagation:** Seed, often planted by birds.
**Uses:** *E. rigida* has an unusual shape that develops better in cultivation than it does in the wild. Its value to birds makes it ideal for a suitable bird garden, where it is best planted in a mixed bush clump. Flowering and fruiting begin in the second year. This shrub's growth rate is about 50 cm per year. Although growing its best in a warm summer with moderate rainfall, *E. rigida* is a great survivor.

**Make changes as your garden grows** A garden is a dynamic, living entity, and as it matures, some changes may be necessary. Be brave enough to alter an aspect of your garden that does not please you. Analyse what you are not happy with in the garden and plan the change.

## Ekebergia pterophylla

**Rock ash**

**Size:** 2–4 x 3–6 m (wild), up to 2 x 3 m (garden)
**Natural habitat:** This species ranges from the Eastern Cape to the east and north of the country. It is localised, being confined to krans edges and other rocky places.
**Growth form:** It is always short and compact, densely evergreen with small, neat, compound leaves, with the lower branches touching the ground so it often appears as a green mound among barren rocks. The flowers are small and white, making a brief display in spring. It bears small berries that are yellow when they mature in late autumn.
**Propagation:** Seed or cuttings.
**Uses:** *Ekebergia* is ideal for a sloping, north-facing rockery where it could make the main feature, or the filling between taller plants. Eventually, it would also make a dense low screen. The age of first fruiting is about five years. It grows slowly in cultivation, about 30 cm per year. *Ekebergia* enjoys a hot summer with moderate rainfall. It could probably cope with high rainfall if on a steep slope. Frost tolerance is moderate.

## Englerodaphne pilosa

**Silky fibre-bush**

**Size:** 2–4 x 2–3 m (wild), up to 3 x 2 m (garden)
**Natural habitat:** This is an endemic, being found only in a temperate damp zone extending from the Eastern Cape, through KwaZulu-Natal to the eastern Escarpment. This shrub is confined to the deep shade of mist-belt forest.
**Growth form:** *Englerodaphne* is either a tiny delicate tree, with a few semi-weeping branches, or may be shrubby. The leaves are very pale green and densely furry. New growth is silver. The flowers are pale yellow tubes, flaring at the mouth, that hang in small bunches.
**Propagation:** *Englerodaphne* has so far been grown only by 'kidnapping' tiny seedlings from forest paths.
**Uses:** It thrives in shade, flowering in its second year. It has not yet been tried in full sun, but its fragile nature suggests that this could be a waste of a rare asset, a plant that actually prefers shade. *Englerodaphne* even grows well beneath an overhanging deck if watered. Growth rate is about 50 cm per year. It must have high rainfall and a temperate summer. It is probably frost-sensitive, but would never encounter it if placed in full shade. It is unlikely to survive drought.

**Your ideal garden** Don't skimp on the planning stage. Before you start buying or planting anything, ask yourself some questions: Do you want peace or riotous colour; a place to sit in or something to look at; a formal garden, or happy informality? Look at many gardens and choose the best bits from each of them for your own garden plan.

## Ephippiocarpa orientalis

**Dwarf toad tree**

**Size:** 1–3 x 1–3 m (wild), up to 2 m (garden)
**Natural habitat:** *Ephippiocarpa* grows naturally in northern Zululand where it is confined to the undergrowth of dune forest.
**Growth form:** It is shrubby and of delicate appearance. Its twigs are green, decorated with white spots. The leaves are a rich dark green. The flowers are quite large, waxy, white, scented and exquisite, and are followed by most curious fruits. These are off-white with green streaks, papery in appearance but rubbery to the touch, generally resembling little forked, under-inflated balloons.
**Propagation:** Seed has been found difficult to germinate in cultivation, although it is easy enough to find seedlings under a parent plant in the wild.
**Uses:** So far *Ephippiocarpa* has been grown only in KwaZulu-Natal coastal gardens where it thrives in half shade. It is a most desirable foliage, flowering and fruiting shrub for a small garden. Growth of transplanted seedlings is fairly slow, although flowering begins at five years and mature size is achieved at about eight. *Ephippiocarpa* is almost certainly very sensitive to frost and drought. It would be worth trying as an indoor container plant.

## Eriosema psoraleoides

**Eriosema**

**Size:** 1–3 x 1–2 m (wild), up to 2 x 1 m (garden)
**Natural habitat:** This species of shrub grows naturally in the warmer parts of the east of South Africa. It occurs in grasslands, often in extensive stands, usually near water or where the water table is high.
**Growth form:** This is a spindly, erect shrub. Its compound leaves are handsome, and each is divided into three leaflets, velvety, with deeply-cut veins. *Eriosema* has yellow pea-shaped flowers that decorate it for several months. There may even be two flowering seasons – one in spring, another in autumn. The fruits are furry tubes, borne in clusters.
**Propagation:** So far *Eriosema* has been cultivated only from a transplanted seedling. However, seed germinates readily, judging from the many offspring that soon appear around the parent plant in cultivation.
**Uses:** *Eriosema* is a bit scrappy to be used as a solo specimen and looks its best when three or more are planted among smaller plants. Flowering begins at two years. Growth is rapid, full size being attained in three years or less. Older specimens are best cut back occasionally to simulate the effect of fire, or can be discarded as the next generation matures. *Eriosema* likes a warm summer with high rainfall.

**Small is also beautiful** It does not matter if an open garden you visit is much larger than yours. There may be a special corner, or a particular area where colour and form have been used cleverly, which you can copy on a smaller scale in your own garden.

## Erythrina acanthocarpa

**Tambookie thorn**

**Size:** 1–2 x 2–3 m (wild), up to 1 x 2 m (garden)
**Natural habitat:** This is a rare species, found naturally in the Queenstown district in the Eastern Cape. It grows in open dry country, sometimes forming thickets.
**Growth form:** It is a small spiny shrub, with a tendency to sprawl. The leaves are divided into three leaflets, bluish, stiff and elegant. The flowers are built to attract birds, being tubular and predominantly red but laced with greenish-yellow. They are exquisite, even by high *Erythrina* standards, and appear in spring. Nectar collects in the bottom of the tubes, attracting sunbirds. The fruits are pretty too: prickly pods that split when mature to reveal the shining red-and-black seeds.
**Propagation:** Cuttings strike fairly easily, August being the ideal time. Seed produces better-shaped trees and germinates well enough if fresh or scarified.
**Uses:** The flowering display is stunning and demands centre stage. It needs a hot dry sunny spot and withstands near-desert conditions. It can tolerate some frost and is easily protected from severe exposure on a north-facing slope backed by rocks. Flowering, which begins in the fourth year, is much more profuse if the plant experiences a cold winter. Growth rate is about 40 cm per year.

## Erythrina zeyheri

**Ploughbreaker**

**Size:** 1 x 1 m (wild), 1 x 1 m (garden)
**Natural habitat:** *E. zeyheri* is found naturally in the high grasslands of the east.
**Growth form:** This is a dwarf shrub that spends much of its life as a large subterranean rootstock. Frost and fire cut it back to below ground level every year. Nevertheless, it is a very striking plant. Large, spiny, stiff and elegant leaves erupt from the soil in spring. A fine floral display then follows in midsummer. The red tubular flowers attract birds. They are borne in spikes, maturing in sequence over an extended period, so some are always in prime condition for the birds. The fruits are pretty too – cylindrical pods that split to reveal large, rock-hard, dull red seeds.
**Propagation:** Seed, which germinates best if fresh, scarified or receives hot water treatment.
**Uses:** In cultivation *E. zeyheri* requires unorthodox treatment. Ideally, it should be grown in a rough lawn that is cut back with a few slashes from a panga each summer. It could be grown in a flowerbed or rockery but must receive full sun, and will suffer if over-watered. It flowers by the second year at the latest. It particularly enjoys a cool or temperate climate inland. It can be grown in winter rainfall, provided drainage is good.

**Birds see red** Red flowers, such as those of *Burchellia*, *Erythrina* and *Leonotis*, are so coloured to attract bird pollinators, as they are able to spot red better than any other colour. The red colour in flowers is due to anthocyanin pigments in acid cell sap.

## Erythroxylum emarginatum

**Common coca tree**

**Size:** 2–6 x 2–5 m (wild), up to 5 x 5 m (garden)
**Natural habitat:** This grows naturally in the warmer, wetter parts of the east. It occurs in evergreen forests, either at the edge or in total shade in the undergrowth, or on rocky outcrops where fire cannot penetrate.
**Growth form:** It is a small tree, often shrubby. The leaves are dark and glossy, the foliage dense. The flowers are small and white, but sweetly scented, and can make a fine display when produced in abundance. The fruits are tiny red plums, sweet and edible. This is the host of the butterfly *Euriphene achlys*.
**Propagation:** Seed.
**Uses:** *Erythroxylum* makes a lovely small specimen. Performance in cultivation depends on the degree of shade. A shade-suppressed specimen grew to 3 m in 12 years. It then filled out tremendously, gained another metre in height, and flowered profusely within two years of being released into full sunshine. Flowering took place in mid-winter, contrary to the normal performance of wild trees. *Erythroxylum* likes a warm summer with moderate to good rainfall. It tolerates an average winter drought. Performance in frost is unknown.

## Eugenia capensis

**Dune myrtle**

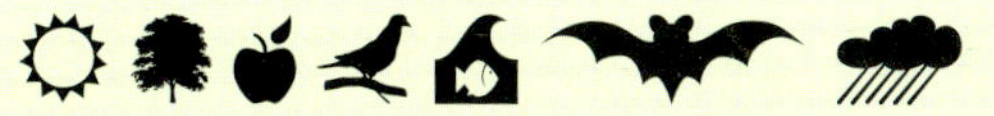

**Size:** 2–3 x 2–3 m (wild), up to 2 x 2 m (garden)
**Natural habitat:** This grows naturally on the coast of the southeast, virtually confined to the seaward side of dune forest.
**Growth form:** It often forms a dense shrubbery between the primary colonisers at the top of the beach and the forest proper. *E. capensis* is compact and the leaves are perfectly round and most attractive. The foliage exudes a rich myrtle smell when crushed. The flowers are white and although fairly small, are borne in masses and make a pleasing display. The fruits resemble small black plums and appear from mid-winter onwards. They have a sweet-sour taste relished by people, birds and fruit bats alike.
**Propagation:** Seed.
**Uses:** *E. capensis* is especially useful at the coast. Once established, it provides shelter for more sensitive plants. It is worth growing for its foliage alone, and because branches are retained at ground level, makes a good screen. Flowering begins at four years. It is also a useful addition to a bird garden within the natural range. Speed of growth is about 40 cm per year. *E. capensis* must have high rainfall, although seems to enjoy a temperate summer as much as the warm summers of its natural range.

**Dune forest** Local conditions will change a forest's composition and structure. An example of this is a 'dune forest', which is situated next to a beach. It contains relatively few shrub species. *Eugenia capensis* and *Ficus burtt-davyi* are typical of dune forest.

## Eugenia natalitia

**Natal myrtle**

**Size:** 4–6 x 3–5 m (wild), up to 3 x 3 m (garden)
**Natural habitat:** This species is found naturally in the warmer parts of KwaZulu-Natal and to the eastern Escarpment. It occurs in the undergrowth of evergreen forests and on krans edges where it looks its best.
**Growth form:** *E. natalitia* is a dense shrub or small low-branching tree. The leaves are glossy and dark, small and neat, and new growth is a brilliant copper. This shrub's foliage exudes a rich myrtle smell when crushed. The flowers are white and, although fairly small, are borne in masses and make a pleasing display. *E. natalitia* is noted for its fruits, which resemble small dark red plums. These have a sweet-sour taste relished by people and birds alike.
**Propagation:** Seed.
**Uses:** It makes a good screen and is worth growing for its foliage and flowers. It is also a useful addition to a bird garden within the natural range, but fruiting is a bit erratic outside it. *E. natalitia* grows well enough in partial shade if conditions are damp, but prefers full sun. First flowering occurs at four years and it grows at about 40 cm per year, thriving in a warm or temperate summer with high or moderate rainfall. It tolerates some frost and an average winter drought.

## Euphorbia grandicornis

**Rhino thorn**

**Size:** 1–2 x 2–5 m (wild), up to 1 x 3 m (garden)
**Natural habitat:** This is a lowveld species, occurring at the edges of thickets in hot, dry spots.
**Growth form:** *Euphorbia* is a spiny succulent with a close, rigid branching pattern. It has very few leaves, and then only in its youth, so that photosynthesis is carried out by the green branches of mature plants. The flower is small and dull yellow. Although of modest beauty, it is much used by bees and other insects. The fruits are red capsules and quite attractive lining up in rows on the angled ridges of the branches.
**Propagation:** Cuttings. Small cuttings are easiest to handle and make the best-shaped specimens. A single branch is ideal. Use gloves or sacking when handling these plants as the latex they ooze when they are cut is unpleasant, and a splash in the eye will be harmful. Cuttings should be left to dry in a cool, shady spot for three days before planting.
**Uses:** *Euphorbia* can be used as a cactus substitute in rockeries and Mexican gardens, or as a form specimen. It is probably one of the world's thorniest plants and makes the ultimate protective barrier. *Euphorbia* revels in the heat and grows best on a north-facing slope. Growth rate is about 50 cm per year given a warm summer with moderate rainfall.

**Telling the difference** *Euphorbia* and cacti are often confused, but they are not related. An easy way to tell them apart is to check the sap. Cacti have clear sap, while that of *Euphorbia* species is thick and white.

## Ficus burtt-davyi

### Veld fig

**Size:** 2–8 x 3–15 m (wild), up to 3 x 6 m (garden)
**Natural habitat:** It is wide-ranging in the south and south-east. It occurs on rock outcrops, at the edges of thick dry scrub and in dune forest, where it can form a single-species stand.
**Growth form:** Much depends upon the immediate environment. Among rocks the branches lurch over the contours like an octopus with more arms than it can manage. In thickets the branches ramble scrambler-fashion, or on coastal dunes it might be an ankle-high ground cover. *F. burtt-davyi* also grows as a multi-stemmed tree. The figs are small and yellow, attracting fruit bats and large birds.
**Propagation:** Seed. This should be extracted from over-ripe or dried-out figs. It must be sown in a tray under glass. Cuttings planted in deep sand in August usually strike.
**Uses:** This species is perfect for a north-facing rockery, even in the smallest garden. It maintains the demeanour of a large bonsai throughout its life. The roots are less vigorous than those of other figs so it can be planted near a wall to evade frost. *F. burtt-davyi* can be trained into a dense hedge that thrives at the head of the beach, one of the few plants that can be so used. It enjoys a warm summer.

## Ficus capreifolia

### Sandpaper fig

**Size:** 3–5 x 5–8 m (wild), up to 4 x 7 m (garden)
**Natural habitat:** This fig is found naturally in Zululand and parts of the eastern Lowveld. It is often common especially alongside rivers that experience heavy floods.
**Growth form:** *F. capreifolia* has a scrappy growth habit, with long branches growing in every direction, interlacing with those of adjacent plants, and often rooting where they touch the ground. The resultant thicket is the favourite haunt of night herons. The leaves are harshly hairy, with the texture of coarse-grade sandpaper. The small orange figs attract birds and fruit bats.
**Propagation:** Seed, extracted from over-ripe or dried-out figs. It must be sown in a tray under glass. Cuttings, trimmed and planted in deep sand in August, root easily.
**Uses:** The branches of this practical and fast-growing plant can reach up to 2 m per year. It never gets very tall because new branches are continuously produced at ground level. It can fringe a stream, cover a pergola capping a bridge over the stream, bind stream banks against floods and invariably recovers after being knocked flat. Interestingly, this shrub's leaves can be used to polish wood. It is frost-sensitive and enjoys a warm summer.

**Roots and all** Weeding is best done by hand while the weeds are still small. Gently pull out the unwanted plants, roots and all. The best time to do this is after rain, when the soil is still damp, or after watering your garden.

## Ficus verruculosa

**Water fig**

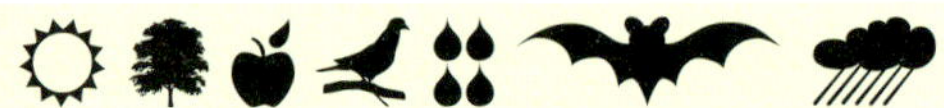

**Size:** 1–3 x 1–3 m (wild), up to 2 x 2 m (garden)
**Natural habitat:** *F. verruculosa* is found naturally in coastal Zululand where it occurs in swamps and wet grassland.
**Growth form:** It tends to be shrubby. This species has the most attractive figs of all. They are a bright deep red when mature and are borne clustered along the smaller branches. The figs are edible and quite sweet. Fruiting occurs twice a year and is usually prolific. The figs appear to be self-fertile, a contrast with other species, all of which require the services of a wasp. Birds enjoy them.
**Propagation:** Seed, which should be extracted from over-ripe or dried-out figs. It must be sown in a tray under glass. Cuttings, which are best trimmed and planted in deep sand during August, strike easily.
**Uses:** In cultivation, *F. verruculosa* is a wonderful subject and is one of the few figs suitable for a small garden. It grows quickly into a rounded shrub. Figs are first produced in the second year, even outside the natural range, when the plant is only 70 cm tall. Although enjoying wet soil, it grows perfectly well under ordinary garden conditions. It likes a warm summer with good rainfall and cannot stand drought, frost or wind.

## Flagellaria guineensis

**Climbing bamboo**

**Size:** 5–25 m long (wild), up to 12 m long (garden)
**Natural habitat:** This is a coastal species, found from the Eastern Cape northwards. It is restricted to evergreen forest.
**Growth form:** *Flagellaria* is a slender but vigorous scrambler, eventually reaching the forest canopy. It resembles slim flexible bamboo. It has beautiful leaf tips that curl into perfect spirals – obvious aids in climbing. The leaves have very finely saw-toothed edges, also a climbing adaptation, but sharp enough to cut the unwary investigator. The fruits are red berries, borne in showy bunches, eaten by birds and monkeys.
**Propagation:** Seed.
**Uses:** *Flagellaria* has two careers in cultivation. As a young plant it makes a great pot plant before it starts to grow its long canes. Later it may get rampant, when it is best incorporated into large screens, binding other plants effectively. It can be added to bushy clumps or trained along a large fence. On a practical level, the canes can be split for making basket-weaving material, combining it with a frame of *Artabotrys* or *Monanthotaxis*. *Flagellaria* grows at least 1 m per year and much more once established. It likes a warm climate with good rainfall.

**Riverine forest** This forest type occurs in strips along major rivers, especially in the lowlands. It is used to a good groundwater supply, often supplied by a far-off catchment. Typical of this habitat are *Ficus capreifolia* and *Mondia whitei*.

## Flueggia virosa

**White berry-bush**

**Size:** 2–4 x 2–4 m (wild), up to 3 x 3 m (garden)
**Natural habitat:** *Flueggia* is found naturally in the warmer parts of the east and occurs in most wooded habitats except evergreen forest.
**Growth form:** It is usually a small spindly tree that may be multi-stemmed. The branching pattern is distinctive, especially in the young plant. Branchlets are stiff and straight, growing upwards at 30°, and arise in a perfect spiral pattern around the parent branch. The spiralling effect is accentuated by the long pale stripes on the reddish bark and the sparseness of the foliage. The leaves are clearly and delicately veined. *Flueggia* is noted for its fruits – masses of white berries that cover the tree.
**Propagation:** Seed.
**Uses:** *Flueggia* makes a pleasant specimen, or could be included in a low-growing thicket. It is too flimsy to make a screen by itself. Fruiting begins at four years within the natural range. However, sexes are separate, so male trees must be included in any garden outside the natural range if the females are to bear fruit. Growth is rapid – up to 1 m per year initially, slowing later as the plant fills out. *Flueggia* must have a warm summer and tolerates moderate drought and a little frost.

## Freylinia lanceolata

**Honey bell bush**

**Size:** 3–6 x 2–4 m (wild), up to 4 x 3 m (garden)
**Natural habitat:** *F. lanceolata* occurs in fynbos regions of the western and southern Cape where it is found along mountain watercourses.
**Growth form:** This is an erect shrub, typically with only a few parallel stems, usually with a lesser spread than height. The leaves are narrow and dark, and the foliage has a willow-like quality. The flowers are little trumpets that are borne abundantly on and off, virtually all year round. They are creamy, with a violet blush and yellow mouth, and have a honey scent.
**Propagation:** Cuttings. Good results are obtained by sacrificing a whole plant, cutting off the whole stem at knee-height. The top makes conventional cuttings. Split the bottom vertically several times, retaining some root on each piece.
**Uses:** This is a most decorative flowering shrub, worth planting as a specimen, or could be used in an informal screen. Flowers first appear at two years. Although found naturally in the winter-rainfall area, *F. lanceolata* grows extremely well in a summer-rainfall regime. In a temperate climate it does not need supplementary watering in winter. Growth rate in cultivation is initially 80 cm per year, slowing after a couple of years.

**'Weedeaters' and shrubs** The 'Weedeater' is a wonderful time-saving device, but beware of it getting too close to your shrubs. The flailing nylon cord can ring-bark a plant in an instant, which can often cause a plant to die.

## Freylinia tropica

### Tropical freylinia

**Size:** 1–3 x 1–2 m (wild), up to 2 x 1 m (garden)
**Natural habitat:** In South Africa, this species is confined to the dry woodlands fringing the southern Kalahari.
**Growth form:** *F. tropica* is an erect shrub, typically with only a few parallel stems, taller than its spread. The leaves are neatly toothed, glossy and dark. The flowers are little trumpets that are borne on and off virtually all year round. They are white, with the faintest hint of violet, the petals having the texture of fine crystals. In KwaZulu-Natal collared sunbirds love them – an unexpected relationship considering their normal geographical separation.
**Propagation:** Cuttings.
**Uses:** This is a most decorative shrub. It is a lovely flowering specimen and the foliage is dense enough to be used in a low screen. Apart from its other fine qualities, *F. tropica* grows extremely well in a large pot. In cultivation, flowers first appear at two years. The growth rate is about 50 cm per year. *F. tropica* withstands an average winter drought.

## Grewia flava

### Brandy bush

**Size:** 2–4 x 2–4 m (wild), up to 2 x 3 m (garden)
**Natural habitat:** *G. flava* is found in the warmer, drier parts of the north. It occurs in grassland and in low-growing thickets.
**Growth form:** It is shrubby and rounded. The leaves are attractive bluish-green above, white below, and the upper surface has the texture of softest velvet. The pretty yellow flowers have a central mass of stamens and the flowering period can last several months. The fruits are small and dull orange. The pips are large and the flesh thin, but the latter has a pleasant flavour not unlike that of dates. Birds find it irresistible.
**Propagation:** Seed, but germination is erratic. Best results come from seed collected from the droppings of wild animals.
**Uses:** *G. flava* makes a pretty shrub. It makes a good screen, although in marginal climates is semi-deciduous and best mixed with *Rhus* or other shrubs. It is ideal for bush clumps or a bird garden. Flowering and fruiting begin in the second year. Growth rate is about 60 cm per year initially, slowing down as the plant thickens out. It likes a warm dry summer and is exceptionally drought-hardy.

**Patience rewards** Nearly all indigenous species are easy to grow, but some, notably most species of *Grewia*, will require different approaches – don't give up too easily as some plants may take up to a year to germinate. With *Grewia*, seeds are best collected from animal droppings (see Introduction), so that they are already processed.

## Grewia flavescens

**Rough-leaved raisin**

**Size:** 3–7 x 2 x 5 m (wild), up to 5 x 3 m (garden)
**Natural habitat:** *G. flavescens* occurs in Zululand and over much of the northeast in dry woodland, often on termite mounds or among rocks.
**Growth form:** It is always shrubby and tends to put out long branches looking for extra support, although it can stand alone. The branches are square in cross-section, the shape becoming accentuated with age as winged ridges develop. The flowers are bright yellow with a central mass of stamens. The flowering period can last several months. The fruits are dull orange. Although the pips are large and the flesh thin, they are tasty and birds love them.
**Propagation:** Seed, but germination is erratic. Best results come from seed collected from the droppings of wild animals.
**Uses:** *G. flavescens* is ideal in bush clumps or a bird garden. It flowers profusely, and in an experimental garden the fruits attracted more birds than any plant. Best results can be expected by accommodating the scrambling habit along a fence. Flowering and fruiting start in the second year. *G. flavescens* makes a good screen, although in marginal climates it is leafless for three months. Growth rate is at least 1 m per year. It likes a warm summer with moderate rainfall.

## Grewia lasiocarpa

**Forest raisin**

**Size:** 3–8 x 3–6 m (wild), up to 5 x 4 m (garden)
**Natural habitat:** This species is fairly widespread in the southeast, and occurs on the edges of evergreen forest.
**Growth form:** It is a solid upright shrub that may scramble if given support. The leaves are large and the foliage dense. The flowers are mauve-pink with a central mass of yellow stamens and are large by *Grewia* standards. The fruits are dull orange when mature and divided into four segments. Fruit crops are regular and heavy. The pips are large and the flesh thin, but the latter has a pleasant flavour not unlike that of dates. Birds find it irresistible.
**Propagation:** Seed, but germination is erratic. Best results come from seed collected from the droppings of wild animals.
**Uses:** *G. lasiocarpa* makes an ideal dense, fast-growing flowering screen. It is never leafless. Flowering and fruiting start in the second year. It is ideal for a bush clump or a bird garden. Its initial growth rate is about 1.2 m per year, subsequently slowing down as it thickens out. *G. lasiocarpa* grows best in areas of high rainfall but can tolerate a normal winter drought.

**Year-round colour** Plan your shrubbery to ensure that you have colour all year round. If space permits, plant more than one of your favourite shrubs, which will link together different areas of the garden.

## Grewia microthyrsa

### Lebombo raisin

**Size:** 3–5 x 2–4 m (wild), up to 3 x 2 m (garden)
**Natural habitat:** *G. microthyrsa* occurs in Zululand and the Lowveld on sandy soils. It is found in fairly thick dry woodland.
**Growth form:** It has a shrubby growth habit but is denser and more upright than most other species of *Grewia*. The flowers are most attractive – pale yellow with a dark yellow central stamen mass. The flowering period can last several months. The fruits resemble little pears and are black when ripe. They do not taste as nice as other *Grewia* fruits but this does not deter birds.
**Propagation:** Seed, but germination is erratic. Best results come from seed collected from the droppings of wild animals.
**Uses:** *G. microthyrsa* makes a pleasant specimen. It is never leafless although thins in a dry winter and is best mixed with other shrubs in a screen. It is ideal in bush clumps or a bird garden. Flowering and fruiting commence in the third year. Growth rate is about 60 cm per year initially, slowing down as the plant thickens out. *G. microthyrsa* likes a warm climate with moderate rainfall. It can tolerate some frost.

## Grewia monticola

### Silver raisin

**Size:** 2–5 x 2–5 m (wild), up to 3 x 3 m (garden)
**Natural habitat:** This is a fairly widespread species, occurring in Zululand and over much of the northeast. It is found in deciduous woodland, often alongside its 'look-alike', *G. hexamita*.
**Growth form:** *G. monticola* is usually shrubby with arching branches. The leaves are the most attractive of all *Grewia* species, being asymmetric to the point of having an 'eared' appearance. The upper surface is bright green, the venation creating a rich texture, and the undersurface is silvery white. There is a short deciduous period in winter. The flowers are yellow, with a central mass of stamens. The flowering period can last several months. The small orange fruits are irresistible to birds, their flesh tasting similar to that of dates.
**Propagation:** Seed, but germination is erratic. Best results come from seed collected from the droppings of wild animals.
**Uses:** *G. monticola* makes a delightful garden shrub and a good screen. It is ideal in bush clumps or a bird garden. Flowering and fruiting commence in the second year. The growth rate is about 50 cm per year. It grows best in a warm climate with moderate rainfall.

**Keep your soil nitrogen-rich** Beware of using unrotted grass cuttings as mulch, as this will rob the soil of nitrogen. The process of decay uses up nitrogen, so unrotted grass cuttings will leach the soil of it. Nitrogen is important, as a lack of it can cause severe yellowing in plants.

## Grewia occidentalis

### Kruisbessie

**Size:** 3–7 x 2–5 m (wild), up to 6 x 4 m (garden)
**Natural habitat:** This is very widespread, being absent only from the arid regions. It occurs on coastal dunes, the edges of evergreen forest, in dry woodland and on high cold koppies.
**Growth form:** It can be a proper tree but is usually an erect multi-stemmed shrub with a tendency to ramble. It is almost evergreen but in cold or dry winters it is briefly deciduous. The flowers are pinkish-mauve with a central mass of yellow stamens. They are produced in profusion and the flowering period can last several months. The fruits are dull orange. The pips are large and the flesh thin but the latter has a pleasant flavour of dates, and birds love it. *G. occidentalis* is host to the skipper butterflies *Netrobalane canopus* and *Eagris nottoana*.
**Propagation:** Seed, but germination is erratic.
**Uses:** *G. occidentalis* makes a good screen, although its rambling habit is best mixed with other shrubs. It is essential in bush clumps or a bird garden. Flowering and fruiting commence in the second year. It grows about 1.5 m per year initially. It enjoys any climate, wet or dry, hot or cold, and is one of the most frost-hardy of all indigenous shrubs.

## Hibiscus pedunculatus

### Pink hibiscus

**Size:** 1–3 x 1–2 m (wild), up to 2 x 1 m (garden)
**Natural habitat:** This species is found naturally on the KwaZulu-Natal coast and the warmer, wetter parts of the Midlands. It occurs at the edges of evergreen forest and sometimes in the forest interior where light penetration is good.
**Growth form:** It is a spindly upright shrub. The foliage is sparse, the leaves lobed and distinctive. The flowers are showy, conical and pink. Some are present almost year-round and are visited by sunbirds.
**Propagation:** Seed. The trick is to harvest it just before the mature dry fruit splits, scattering the lot. Cuttings strike easily, even when stuck into unprepared ground.
**Uses:** *H. pedunculatus* makes a lovely flowering shrub and looks its best if massed in a little grove. It flowers and reaches mature size after about two years and can be pruned into a delicate miniature standard if it gets too straggly. Alternatively, older plants can be pulled out, provided that self-seeding is taking place. *H. pedunculatus* enjoys a warm summer with moderate to good rainfall and can only stand short droughts. It prefers full sunshine but grows well enough in dappled shade. Frost tolerance is slight.

**Don't over-tidy** Fallen leaves provide natural mulch. Guard against being too tidy by picking up every fallen leaf, because you could create a rather sterile garden. Many harmless little creatures live in leaf litter.

## Hibiscus tiliaceus

**Lagoon hibiscus**

**Size:** 3–6 x 4–9 m (wild), up to 4 x 6 m (garden)
**Natural habitat:** *H. tiliaceus* is found naturally on the coast, from about East London northwards. It invariably occurs in estuaries, where it may form a dense fringe just above the high-tide mark, and in swamp forests.
**Growth form:** It is multi-stemmed, the branches forming a dense tangle. The leaves are very handsome, large and heart-shaped, with a greyish tinge. The flowers too are outstanding, large, bright pale yellow, later turning orange or even red before they fall. The centre of the flower is deep maroon. The seeds are dispersed by water, floating naturally for six months and more.
**Propagation:** Seed. Harvest it just before the mature dry fruit splits, scattering the lot. Cuttings strike easily.
**Uses:** *H. tiliaceus* makes a striking if unconventional specimen, given enough space, and is particularly attractive next to water. It is one of the fastest growing indigenous shrubs, achieving up to 2 m per year initially. Flowering begins in the second year. It also makes an impenetrable screen. *H. tiliaceus* thrives on or near the southeastern coast, but need not be planted in a damp spot. Inland it languishes through droughts and must be given a wet sunny position.

## Hoslundia opposita

**Orange bird-berry**

**Size:** 1–2 x 1–2 m (wild), up to 1 x 1 m (garden)
**Natural habitat:** *Hoslundia* ranges from the warmer parts of much of the east to the south coast of KwaZulu-Natal. It grows in grassland and open woodland.
**Growth form:** There are two growth forms; an upright form, better for the small garden, and the creeping form from Zululand. *Hoslundia* is evergreen with dense foliage. Leaves are pale green and, like other members of the mint family, have a crisp smell when crushed. The flowers are minute but attractive to butterflies. Chameleons often lie in ambush just under the flower heads. The soft orange 'fruits' are actually swollen calyxes. They glow in contrast with the foliage. *Hoslundia* is one of the best bird-attracting fruits of all, much loved by bulbuls.
**Propagation:** Seed. Semi-hardwood cuttings also root easily.
**Uses:** *Hoslundia* makes a perfect foliage and fruiting specimen for a small garden. Plant several around a bird bath: the dense mat of intertwined branches prevents cats from attacking birds. It can be regularly cut back, but never remove more than a quarter of the foliage at once. *Hoslundia* grows to full size within two years. It likes a warm summer with at least moderate rainfall.

**Make your own compost** Every garden should have a corner where compost can be made. Use vegetable peelings and fruit waste from the kitchen, weeds, and soft, spent plants. The addition of animal manure will speed up the decomposition process.

## Hyperacanthus amoenus

### Spiny gardenia

**Size:** 3–8 x 2–5 m (wild), up to 5 x 4 m (garden)
**Natural habitat:** This species ranges from the Eastern Cape through the warmer parts of the east and north of South Africa. It is locally common in evergreen forests and on krans edges.
**Growth form:** A specimen grown in the open is upright and slender but if surrounded by thick vegetation *Hyperacanthus* tends to ramble and produce long pendent branches. The leaves are glossy and bursts of new red growth appear almost throughout the year. The branching pattern is perfectly right-angled and the branches bear fierce spines. The flowers are quite large trumpets, pale red with a white interior. They have a strong sweet scent. The large leathery fruits contain many seeds embedded in a mass of fibres.
**Propagation:** Seed, best collected from over-ripe, fallen fruit.
**Uses:** *Hyperacanthus* makes a fine form, foliage and flowering specimen. Flowering begins at three years and is very reliable subsequently. Growth rate is about 50 cm per year. *Hyperacanthus* likes a temperate or warm summer and moderate to good rainfall. It survives considerable drought, however. A cut branch makes an acceptable Christmas tree, being custom-built to enable the maximum number of decorations and presents to be hung upon it.

## Hypericum revolutum

### Curry bush

**Size:** 1–3 x 1–3 m (wild), up to 2 x 2 m (garden)
**Natural habitat:** *Hypericum* is found naturally in the cooler, damper parts of the east and north. It occurs in scrub forest and in damp grassland provided that there have been no fires for some time.
**Growth form:** It is a rounded bush with dense foliage. The foliage always has a fresh appearance and contrasts nicely with the reddish bark. The latter always has insectivorous birds picking over it. The tiny leaves give off a subtly sweet spicy smell when crushed; at certain times the bush exudes the same scent all by itself. However, the oft-quoted comparison with curry is a bit far-fetched. The flowers are cheerful and pretty, with large yellow stars with a powder-puff mass of stamens in the centre.
**Propagation:** Cuttings.
**Uses:** *Hypericum* is worth its place as a specimen shrub or could be used as a hedge. It fits easily into a small garden. Flowering begins at two years and full size is achieved at four to five years. Mature plants flower almost continuously. This shrub is most at home in a temperate summer with moderate to good rainfall but tolerates nearly everything else except for extended drought and heavy frost.

**Improving soil fertility** The addition of compost to soil acts as a mulch, which retains moisture, lightens clay soils, adds body to sandy soils and encourages the presence of earthworms and micro-organisms that make the soil more fertile.

## Indigofera frutescens

River indigo

**Size:** 1–4 x 1–3 m (wild), up to 3 x 2 m (garden)
**Natural habitat:** This species occurs along the coasts of KwaZulu-Natal and the Eastern Cape on forest edges and among low-growing scrub.
**Growth form:** It is an upright slender shrub. The branches form gentle arcs spreading in all directions and bear delicate compound leaves. The flowers are very pretty, pea-like in design, and borne in pyramid-shaped sprays. They are pink and the flowering period lasts three to four months. The fruit is a thin pod that splits and twists open when dry.
**Propagation:** Seed.
**Uses:** *I. frutescens* is very reliable in the garden. Because of its small size and delicate appearance it is best used in a flowerbed or on the sunny edge of a shrubbery. Flowering begins in the first year and is profuse by the second year. Individual flowers have a long life even when cut and used in floral arrangements. *I. frutescens* grows 1 m or more for the first two years, thickening out thereafter. It enjoys a warm summer with moderate to high rainfall. It is fairly frost-sensitive but this is no problem because it is small enough to be tucked into safe, north-facing corners.

## Indigofera micrantha

Fern indigo

**Size:** 1–2 x 1–2 m (wild), up to 1 x 1.5 m (garden)
**Natural habitat:** *I. micrantha* is found in KwaZulu-Natal on the margins of warm evergreen forests.
**Growth form:** This is a delicate, almost ethereal plant. The leaves are exceptionally pretty, with the best qualities of a maidenhair fern. On any one branch all the leaves are borne exactly in the same plane, creating a striking layered effect. The flowers are lovely, pea-like in design, and borne in pyramid-shaped sprays. They are small and white, bright spangles among the foliage for most of the year.
**Propagation:** Seed.
**Uses:** Because of its exquisite and delicate appearance *I. micrantha* is wasted unless used in a prime flowerbed or close to the stoep. Flowering begins in the first year. The flowering period lasts three to four months and individual flowers have a long life. In cultivation, *I. micrantha* grows well enough in partial shade. However, a potted specimen left accidentally in hot sun for several weeks recovered fully after defoliation and is now a drought-hardy sunshine addict. *I. micrantha* enjoys a warm summer with moderate to high rainfall. Protect it from frost by tucking it into safe, north-facing corners.

**Killing weed seeds** Make sure your compost heap is tall, so that enough decomposition heat is generated in the centre to destroy the seeds of weeds. Place seeding weeds in the centre of your compost heap. Otherwise, put these plants into bags and send them to the dump.

## Jasminum multipartitum

**Wild jasmine**

**Size:** 2–5 x 2–3 m (wild), up to 4 x 3 m (garden)
**Natural habitat:** This grows naturally in the warm dry parts of the east and north. It occurs in deciduous woodland, often among rocks on north-facing slopes.
**Growth form:** *Jasminum* is a modest scrambler that tends to grow up through thick bush patches, pushing out long branches through the edges. The leaves are small and wavy and make a pleasant show. They thin out in an average winter. The flowers appear in spring and are extremely beautiful. Before they open they stand up like pink candles. Mature flowers are white stars with a strong sweet smell, borne in cascades that cover the supporting bushes.
**Propagation:** Cuttings.
**Uses:** If grown as a specimen, *Jasminum* twines around on itself, eventually producing a shrub of sorts. It is better planted next to a stiffly-branching small tree such as *Dichrostachys* or *Grewia occidentalis*, or against a fence or trellis, where it can better display its talents. It mixes well into a low shrubbery. Growth in cultivation is rapid, at least 1 m per year, and flowering begins at two years. *Jasminum* tolerates a wide range of climates.

## Karomia speciosa

**Wild parasol flower**

**Size:** 2–7 x 1–4 m (wild), up to 5 x 3 m (garden)
**Natural habitat:** *Karomia* is found naturally in Zululand and the eastern Lowveld where it occurs on hot dry rocky hills. It is best seen in the Kruger Park just within the Phalaborwa Gate.
**Growth form:** It tends to be multi-stemmed but appears tree-like because all stems are swept upwards and fairly tightly packed in the style of some poplars. *Karomia* may be briefly deciduous in a dry winter. The flowers are attractive and unusual, with deep violet corollas peeping out of pale lilac star-shaped calyxes. A related Indian species gets the name 'Chinese hat' from this feature. Flowering continues virtually throughout the year.
**Propagation:** Cuttings.
**Uses:** *Karomia* is well known in gardens, probably because its great drought hardiness enables it to survive total neglect. It is pretty enough to be used as a flowering specimen and its shape adds texture to a shrubbery, as well as allowing it to fit into a small garden. It begins flowering in the second year. Growth is reasonably quick, about 60 cm per year. *Karomia* thrives in most climates but has yet to be tested in hard frost.

**Hardy autumn leaves** Grass cuttings and autumn leaves take a long time to decompose and should be kept separate from the rest of the compost material. Keep the layers thin and add lots of animal manure to assist decomposition.

## Keetia gueinzii

**Climbing canthium**

**Size:** 4–20 x 3–12 m (wild), up to 9 x 5 m (garden)
**Natural habitat:** *Keetia* is a forest dweller from KwaZulu-Natal and the eastern Escarpment. It is common in coastal forest, less so in the mist-belt.
**Growth form:** In the wild it is always a scrambler, and mature plants send long branches up through the forest canopy and outwards from the forest edges. Young plants have a right-angled branching habit, lost with age. Great sprays of white flowers cascade out of the forest in early summer. *Keetia* also produces great quantities of fruit, an important food for birds. This is black and shiny when ripe but the whole crop is often consumed by birds while still green.
**Propagation:** Seed.
**Uses:** *Keetia* is ideal for a bird garden, bush clump or screen. If planted in isolation it grows first as a dense bush but soon sends out a few exploratory branches. When these make contact with support they lengthen rapidly and scramble so *Keetia* is best planted beside a fence where it can grow to best advantage and provide a useful screen. First flowering occurs at three years. It grows over 1 m per year. It grows best in a warm environment with moderate to good rainfall.

## Kraussia floribunda

**Kraussia**

**Size:** 2–5 x 2–5 m (wild), up to 3 x 3 m (garden)
**Natural habitat:** *Kraussia* is found naturally in the warmer, wetter parts of the east. It occurs in evergreen forests and may dominate the undergrowth of riverine or swamp forests.
**Growth form:** It is upright but always shrubby. The foliage is glossy and dark. *Kraussia* has pretty white flowers that appear for an extended period in midsummer. These are followed by a profusion of black berries, peaking in mid-winter, which are enjoyed by people and birds alike.
**Propagation:** Seed.
**Uses:** *Kraussia* is an ideal garden subject and is by no means as demanding as its specialised natural habitat would suggest. It makes a pleasing specimen or can be mixed with other species in a flowering screen and informal bird garden. Flowering and fruiting occur at two years, and regularly thereafter. Although it likes partial shade *Kraussia* performs much better if given full sun. Provided that the summer is warm, it tolerates poor rainfall even where the soil is dry and slightly alkaline. Even under these conditions it grows about 60 cm per year and considerably faster where rainfall is high. Its tolerance to frost is unknown but likely to be slight at best. *Kraussia* thrives in a pot.

**Replenishing soil** There is no limit to the amount of compost that can be added to the garden. The soil is continually being impoverished by plants taking up nourishment. Moreover, excessive watering leaches out essential minerals in the soil; compost replaces some of these.

## Landolphia kirkii

**Landolphia**

**Size:** 10–40 m long (wild), up to 18 m (garden)
**Natural habitat:** *Landolphia* is confined to tall forest in Zululand and the eastern Lowveld.
**Growth form:** It is a rampant creeper, a beanstalk of which Jack would have been proud. Young tendrils curl in all directions. Later, plants twist around everything within reach. Those that outlive their supports and crash to the forest floor soon writhe back into the sunshine. The bark is smooth and adorned with white pores: these give delicacy to a young shoot and crusty character to old trunks. The foliage is brilliantly glossy, sometimes sealing the forest edge with hanging curtains. The flowers are little white stars. *Landolphia* has showy, large and round, yellow fruits. The shell is easily broken open, revealing a gaudy orange pulp with a sharp taste.
**Propagation:** Seed.
**Uses:** *Landolphia* is a fine embellishment for a strong fence or large pergola. In a warm wet climate the growth rate is at least 3 m per year. Growth is slower if conditions are dry, although the beautiful foliage gloss and stem formations are the same. Flowers appear at four years. Fruiting has not so far been seen outside the natural range. An exquisite jelly can be made from the fruits.

## Leonotis leonurus

**Wild dagga**

**Size:** 2–3 x 1–2 m (wild), up to 3 x 2 m (garden)
**Natural habitat:** *Leonotis* is found naturally in the eastern grasslands, occurring at most altitudes.
**Growth form:** It is a slender upright shrub. Although perennial, it has some characteristics of an annual since every winter it is either frosted or burnt back to ground level, beginning life anew in spring. The orange tubular flowers appear in early autumn, developing in whorls on every stem. As the first whorl matures, new whorls are growing in sequence above it and eventually six to eight may be produced. So the flowering period lasts four to six weeks and there are always flowers in the right condition for hosts of itinerant sunbirds.
**Propagation:** Seed. *Leonotis* self-seeds readily and one plant will produce a little colony in a few years.
**Uses:** This shrub is a reliable flowering specimen in almost every climate, provided it has full sun all day. The ideal is to plant a small patch about 10 m away from the stoep, where visiting birds can be watched from an armchair. Once flowering and seeding are complete, it should be pruned down to 30 to 40 cm to simulate frost or fire. Unpruned plants get straggly and flower less well. It is especially valuable in very frosty areas.

**No relation** *Leonotis leonurus* has the strange common name of wild dagga. This is a complete misnomer, as it is not related to *Cannabis*, the dagga plant. No part of *L. leonurus* is used as a hallucinogenic drug.

## Leptactina delagoensis

### Leptactina

**Size:** 1–4 x 1–3 m (wild), up to 3 x 2 m (garden)
**Natural habitat:** This grows naturally in Zululand. It is found in sand forest, particularly on the margins, and is locally common at False Bay, St Lucia.
**Growth form:** *Leptactina* is an upright shrub with a tendency to scramble if there is any support. The foliage is glossy and the leaf veins form a neat V-pattern as they point diagonally forward. This shrub is more or less evergreen. It has quite exceptionally beautiful flowers – fragrant snow-white stars, which appear in spring.
**Propagation:** Fruit is difficult to find, and so far *Leptactina* has been cultivated mainly from seedlings found beneath a parent plant. Cuttings have limited success.
**Uses:** This is a most rewarding plant, for it flowers well in half shade or in even darker conditions, provided that it gets an hour or so of sunshine each day. Growth rate is modest, about 30 cm per year, but flowering begins at two years. *Leptactina* likes a warm summer and tolerates an average winter drought. This shrub is probably frost-sensitive, but this should not be much of a problem, since it is small enough to be planted in a sheltered spot.

## Leucadendron uliginosum

### Outeniqua conebush

**Size:** up to 2.3 x 1 m (wild), up to 2 x 1.5 m (garden)
**Natural habitat:** It occurs in the fynbos on the mountains surrounding Knysna in the southern Cape.
**Growth form:** *L. uliginosum* exists in two forms; the subspecies *uliginosum* is considered here. It is a slender shrub, forking low down, but the branches are held erect. It has arguably the finest foliage of any shrub. The leaves are a pale silvery green, with the appearance and feel of silken steel. Leaves on upper branches press tightly against the pink bark, some of which is exposed, producing a striking mosaic. Branch tips curl in snake-like fashion. Sexes are separate. Male flowers are yellow. Female flowers form a tight cone that appears silver, pink or green, depending on the play of light.
**Propagation:** Seed, which should be given a warm soaking; cuttings, best taken in February.
**Uses:** The leaf and branch form make it ideal for a 'braille trail'. The leaves are at their best virtually year-round and last well in cut flower arrangements. Flowering begins at two years within the natural range, at three elsewhere. Growth rate is about 40 cm per year. *L. uliginosum* must be cut often, especially when young. Unpruned plants get straggly. It grows best in a temperate climate with good rainfall and regular breezes.

**A haven for birds** Leaf litter that collects naturally under your shrubs provides a perfect environment for ground-feeding birds such as robins and thrushes. They will happily scuffle through the leaves and find all sorts of tasty morsels.

## Leucospermum cordifolium

### Pincushion

**Size:** up to 1.5 x 3 m (wild), up to 2.5 x 5 m (garden)
**Natural habitat:** It occurs in the southwestern Cape between the Kogelberg and Bredasdorp, growing on sandy lowlands.
**Growth form:** *L. cordifolium* is always shrubby, with spreading, drooping branches producing a fairly neat, rounded shape. The flower heads are stunning, very large and bright orange, or sometimes yellow or red, in colour. The styles stick up in a mass, creating the pincushion effect. Flowering lasts about two months over spring and the plant seems weighed to the ground with flowers. Sunbirds and sugarbirds love them.
**Propagation:** Seed, but germination is rather poor; cuttings, best taken in January.
**Uses:** *L. cordifolium* makes a fabulous flowering specimen and bird garden plant. Pruning is not essential because old flower heads fall off anyway. To improve branching and the number of flowering shoots, always prune above the lowermost leaves and axillary buds. If the cut is lower, the whole branch will die. Flowering begins at three years. Flowers are best picked after half the styles have emerged. Cut flowers last well. *L. cordifolium* survives about 10 years, so plant the next generation in time to maintain continuity. It likes a temperate climate with good rainfall and regular breezes.

## Lippia javanica

### Lippia

**Size:** 2–3 x 1–2 m (wild), up to 2 x 2 m (garden)
**Natural habitat:** *Lippia* is found naturally in much of the east and north. It occurs in all grasslands except at higher altitudes, being common – even dominant – where over-grazing is prevalent. Large herbivores eat just about everything else first. For this reason it is often condemned as a weed.
**Growth form:** *Lippia* is a slim upright shrub. The leaves are unremarkable to look at but when crushed are noted for their crisp and stinging but pleasant scent. Walkers brushing past *Lippia* will be aware of this. It bears modest white flowers.
**Propagation:** Seed.
**Uses:** *Lippia* is not a conventional garden plant but is well worth a place where scent is the theme. It could line a pathway, where garden visitors are bound to experience it, or be grown in a flowerbed without interfering with anything else. Mosquitoes are repelled by it, even by a cut branch hung over an evening outdoor picnic, so it may be worth planting a small thicket to ensure supplies. *Lippia* grows at least 1 m per year, attaining full size at three years. It grows well in almost any climate.

**A pick-me-up** Plant *Lippia javanica* at the edge of a path or walkway so that you can pick and smell a piece whenever you walk by. Its crisp, sharp smell will provide you with an instant pick-me-up.

## Ludwigia octovalvis

### Ludwigia

**Size:** 1–3 x 1–2 m (wild), up to 2 x 1 m (garden)
**Natural habitat:** *Ludwigia* is quite widespread in the east and north. It is a strictly aquatic shrub, always found at the edge of ponds or permanent marshes, even with some roots actually in the water.
**Growth form:** *Ludwigia* is a slender shrub. Little pinkish breathing roots protrude from the mud all around it, mangrove style. The young twigs are purple, complementing the very beautiful leaves that are densely furry, strikingly veined and nearly always display red new growth. The flowers are yellow cups and are present throughout summer.
**Propagation:** *Ludwigia* is best grown directly from seed in the desired spot. The seeds are as fine as dust and when scattered on a pond surface will be quickly blown to the ideal germination spot by the wind.
**Uses:** *Ludwigia* is ideal for the damp margins of a pond. It grows in almost any climate provided its pond is maintained. Full height is attained within a year. Thereafter it thickens a little or may die within two years. This is not a problem as it self-seeds once established – quite fun because the location of the colony varies from year to year, depending on the wind direction on germination day.

## Lycium acutifolium

### Wolwedoring

**Size:** 1–4 x 1–2 m (wild), up to 3 x 2 m (garden)
**Natural habitat:** *Lycium* is found naturally in the warmer parts of the Eastern Cape and KwaZulu-Natal. It usually grows in low scrub, often near the high-water mark.
**Growth form:** It is shrubby, with a tendency to scramble if there is anything to lean against. *Lycium* is spiny, and older specimens have attractive fissured bark. The tiny neat leaves are very dark. Young plants may have a deciduous period but after about four years *Lycium* is never leafless. The flowers are pretty, small white or pale violet stars which appear in spring. The fruits are miniature red plums, relished by birds.
**Propagation:** Seed.
**Uses:** *Lycium* mixes well in a bush clump and is ideal for planting against a fence. It makes a complete screen without ever getting too tall, as after two years or so it thickens and grows outwards rather than upwards. It is ideal for a bird garden, especially in dry areas with a hot summer and cold winter. Growth is quick – at least 1 m per year – and first flowering occurs at two years. Fruiting has not so far been seen beyond the natural habitat. *Lycium* tolerates fairly heavy drought and moderate frost.

**Seeds in the veld** If you find a shrub in the veld that appeals to you, try to collect some fresh seed and grow it at home. There is seldom any legal restriction on this type of collection besides obtaining the landowner's permission.

## Mackaya bella

**Mackaya**

**Size:** 1–4 x 1–4 m (wild), up to 3 x 3 m (garden)
**Natural habitat:** *Mackaya* is found naturally in the wetter parts of the east. It occurs in coastal and mist-belt forest, often in the undergrowth.
**Growth form:** *Mackaya* is usually shrubby and densely evergreen. The leaves are large and brilliant, dark and neatly serrated. *Mackaya* is deservedly famed for the beauty of its flowers. These are quite large and a very pale mauve, striped with purple inside. They appear in profusion in spring, sometimes dominating along the edges of forests.
**Propagation:** Cuttings.
**Uses:** *Mackaya* makes a sparkling large shrub and is always worth planting where the climate is suitable. While flowering best where it gets several hours of sun each day, it also enjoys partial shade. An ideal position is the east side of a wall, tall tree or forest clump. Growth is fast, 1 m or so per year, and first flowering occurs at two years. *Mackaya* makes a good screen for a shady position where other plants would struggle. It enjoys a warm summer provided that the rainfall is high; if the summer is temperate it can manage with moderate rainfall. *Mackaya* has little frost tolerance but if planted in the proper place this is never a problem.

## Maerua cafra

**Bush-cherry**

**Size:** 2–6 x 2–5 m (wild), up to 3 x 3 m (garden)
**Natural habitat:** This species ranges from the Eastern Cape through much of the warmer parts of the east and north. It occurs in all sorts of habitats, including deciduous woodland, dune forest and on the fringes of coastal lowland forest.
**Growth form:** It may be shrubby or a small tree. The leaves are very pretty, compound with three or more leaflets. There is a short deciduous period in a marginal climate. The flowers are large and white, consisting mainly of stamens about 3 cm long that stick up vertically, making a fine display in spring. Sunbirds often visit them. The fruit is an irregular tube, eventually going soft and turning orange. *M. cafra* is host to butterflies of the genera *Colotis* and *Belenois*.
**Propagation:** Seed, but the young plant must not be kept in a pot for too long. The root develops very quickly and the plant grows best if planted out as soon as possible.
**Uses:** Given a warm summer with moderate to good rainfall, *M. cafra* makes an ideal small specimen. Growth rate is moderate, about 40 cm per year, but flowering and fruiting begin at three years. It tolerates moderate frost.

**Seedlings from the veld** You can often find seedlings popping up around a parent plant in the wild. These can easily be lifted out by hand after rain and transplanted. The smaller the seedling, the better its chances of survival. Larger, established plants must be left as breeding stock, as they don't transplant well.

## Maerua rosmarinoides

**Needle-leaved bush-cherry**

**Size:** 2–4 x 2–3 m (wild), up to 2 x 2 m (garden)
**Natural habitat:** *M. rosmarinoides* is found naturally in much of KwaZulu-Natal, just extending into the southeastern part of Mpumalanga. It occurs sparingly in a variety of habitats, particularly deciduous woodland and sand forest.
**Growth form:** It may be shrubby, or a small tree, or may scramble if crowded. It tends to have a 'weeping' habit. This, coupled with the fine, almost needle-like leaflets reminiscent of the rosemary herb, creates a Japanese impression. The flowers are white and consist mainly of vertical stamens of about 2 cm, making a fine display in spring. The fruit is a thin bean, beaded around the seeds.
**Propagation:** Seed, but the seedling must be planted out quickly. Roots develop very quickly and the plant grows best if planted out as soon as possible. Cuttings strike well.
**Uses:** *M. rosmarinoides* makes an exquisite small specimen well worth a prime spot. Flowering normally begins in the second year but results are not guaranteed. One specimen struggled for 15 years in a variety of 'wrong' positions, shrinking in the process. Finally – perhaps because new roots had formed – it raced away at 70 cm per year. *M. rosmarinoides* likes a warm summer with moderate rainfall.

## Maesa lanceolata

**Maesa**

**Size:** 3–5 x 3–5 m (wild), up to 3 x 4 m (garden)
**Natural habitat:** *Maesa* is indigenous to the wetter parts of KwaZulu-Natal and the far northeast. It occurs at forest edges and alongside streams in open grassland. This shrub rapidly takes over cleared areas and will spring up in damp grassland in the absence of fire.
**Growth form:** It is rather a scruffy large shrub or small tree that branches low down. *Maesa* has small white flowers that make quite a display, always abuzz with bees and other insects. The timing depends on the rains: in a wet year flowering occurs in early summer; in dry years, later. It is a prolific fruit-bearer, producing big clusters of snow-white berries. These are the favourite food of starlings and other birds too, but reputedly poisonous to humans.
**Propagation:** Seed.
**Uses:** *Maesa* is not a conventional garden beauty; it is best used in a mixed informal screen where quick cover is needed, especially when attracting birds. Given a warm or temperate summer with high rainfall it grows about 1.5 m per year. Fruiting begins at two years. On a large scale it can be used as a precursor in the re-establishment of mist-belt forest, providing the initial shelter needed by longer-lived trees.

**Remove seeds from fruit** With many plants, to get their seed, you have to anticipate foraging birds and pick the fruit while not yet fully mature. Separate the seed from the flesh before it becomes mouldy, as the fungus can kill the seeds. The moisture retained by soft fruit may also trigger seed germination before it is planted in a suitable bed.

## Maytenus bachmannii

### Willow maytenus

**Size:** 1–3 x 1–3 m (wild), up to 1.5 x 1.5 m (garden)
**Natural habitat:** This is restricted to Pondoland sandstone in southern KwaZulu-Natal. It is found in the undergrowth of evergreen forest, usually on stream banks.
**Growth form:** It is a compact shrub and retains its foliage to ground level. The small leaves are exquisite: glossy, finely scalloped, contrasting wonderfully with the bright red twigs. The flowers are the best of the genus – tiny white stars. They are small but are borne in masses, producing a pleasing display. They have a musty but not unpleasant smell and are a favourite of bees and other insects. The fruit is a small dull-coloured capsule which splits into three when mature, revealing orange seeds that attract birds.
**Propagation:** Seed.
**Uses:** *M. bachmannii* is an asset in any garden and grows well in a container. It attains mature size at about four years, but flowering begins at two years and an established plant flowers continuously for six months. Garden plants produce fruit outside the natural range. Frost tolerance is not known, but its small size enables it to be easily protected and it thrives in the Johannesburg area, for example. It is not particularly drought-hardy and may need extra water in a dry climate.

## Maytenus mossambicensis

### Red forest spike-thorn

**Size:** 2–4 x 2–4 m (wild), up to 2 x 2 m (garden)
**Natural habitat:** *M. mossambicensis* occurs naturally in the Eastern Cape through to the wetter parts of the east and north. It occurs mainly in evergreen forest and frequently dominates the shrub layer in mist-belt forest.
**Growth form:** It is a spiny evergreen shrub. The leaves are glossy and neatly serrate. The flowers are small and white but borne in masses, producing a lovely display. They have a musty but not unpleasant smell and are a favourite of bees and other insects. The fruit is a small dull-coloured capsule which splits into three when mature, revealing orange or red seeds that attract birds.
**Propagation:** Seed.
**Uses:** This is an attractive species in cultivation and may flower at two years. It makes a good screen and has a rugged charm. Although virtually confined to the shade in the wild, it revels in full sun, growing thicker than usual and glittering in bright light. Growth rate is about 50 cm per year. It grows best if rainfall is high or moderate but tolerates moderate drought.

**Planting in seed trays** Plant seeds to a depth equal to their own size in a friable seedling mix with good drainage. Don't over-water, as this can lead to rotting, and protect the seed trays from the hot sun.

## Maytenus procumbens

**Dune kokoboom**

**Size:** 3–6 x 3–5 m (wild), up to 4 x 3 m (garden)

**Natural habitat:** This is a coastal species, occurring from the southern Cape to northern Zululand. It is more or less confined to dune forest, where it is common in places.

**Growth form:** *M. procumbens* is evergreen and usually shrubby, with a tendency towards a 'weeping' growth habit. The leaves are glossy and almost round. The flowers are small and white but borne in masses, producing a pleasing display. They have a musty but not unpleasant smell and are a favourite of bees and other insects. The fruit is a small dull-coloured capsule which splits into three when mature, revealing orange or red seeds that attract birds.

**Propagation:** Seed.

**Uses:** This is a very useful species at the coast because of its ability to withstand and exclude strong seawinds. It is not first in the beauty league but makes a good screen and has a rugged charm. It is also worth growing for its value to wildlife. Growth rate is about 50 cm per year. *M. procumbens* likes a warm summer with moderate to good rainfall. Frost tolerance is unknown.

## Melianthus comosus

**Small melianthus**

**Size:** 2–3 x 2–3 m (wild), up to 2 x 2 m (garden)

**Natural habitat:** This species ranges from the southern Cape, through the Karoo, to the western Free State. Although most common along watercourses, it also grows in dry scrub.

**Growth form:** This is a small shrub, with a few upright stems. The large compound leaves are very handsome with neatly serrate leaflets. The flowers too are decorative, straw-yellow and red in colour and, being among the most prolific of all nectar producers, are a source of interest to sunbirds. The fruits are papery structures. They split in mid-winter when dry, revealing shiny, spherical black seeds.

**Propagation:** Seed.

**Uses:** *M. comosus* looks its best in full sun among lower-growing plants, especially beside water. Because it branches sparsely it does not make a good screen. Flowering begins in the second year and lasts for a month or more each summer. Its flowers are not as flamboyant as those of its relatives, but *M. comosus* grows and flowers well in slight shade. Growth is rapid – about 1 m per year – so that mature size is attained after two to three years. Thereafter it begins to sprawl and is best kept in shape by pruning. It sprouts in spring even when frosted back.

**Mulching** This is an excellent way to keep the ground moist while at the same time limiting the growth of weeds in your garden. A 5-cm layer of well-rotted compost, decayed leaves or leaf mould is ideal.

## Melianthus major

### Large melianthus

**Size:** 2–3 x 2–3 m (wild), up to 2 x 2 m (garden)
**Natural habitat:** *M. major* grows naturally in the Cape, along rocky watercourses, especially in semi-arid areas.
**Growth form:** It is a multi-stemmed shrub. The striking blue-green leaves are very handsome, large and compound, with neatly serrate leaflets. The flowers are a decorative, brick-red and, being among the most prolific of all nectar producers, are a source of interest to sunbirds. The fruits are papery structures, borne in a spike. They split in mid-winter when dry, revealing large, shiny, spherical black seeds.
**Propagation:** Seed.
**Uses:** *M. major* looks its best in full sun beside water. Flowering begins in the second year and lasts for several months each summer. Because it branches sparsely, *M. major* does not make a good screen. Growth is rapid – about 1 m per year. Thereafter it begins to sprawl and is best kept in shape by pruning. The foliage is sometimes eaten by big caterpillars and grasshoppers. If necessary, remove them by hand; sprays will affect all the visiting birds. Despite occurring in dry areas in the wild, *M. major* withstands only short droughts in the garden. It withstands considerable frost and usually sprouts in spring even when frosted back.

## Melianthus villosus

### Berg melianthus

**Size:** 1–2 x 1–2 m (wild), up to 1.5 x 1.5 m (garden)
**Natural habitat:** This is found naturally in the Drakensberg of KwaZulu-Natal and the Free State, where it grows beside streams and in other damp spots.
**Growth form:** This is a small multi-stemmed shrub. The leaves are very handsome, large and compound, with neatly serrate leaflets. The decorative brick-red flowers attract sunbirds. The fruits are tall, papery structures, borne in a spike. They split in mid-winter when dry, revealing large, shiny, spherical black seeds.
**Propagation:** Seed.
**Uses:** *M. villosus* looks its best in full sun beside water. Plant three or more plants together for full effect. Flowering begins in the second year and lasts for a month or more each summer. Because it branches sparsely *M. villosus* does not make a good screen. In cultivation it is particularly susceptible to drought; even a brief hot dry spell will kill it. Growth is rapid – about 1 m per year. Thereafter, it begins to sprawl and is best kept in shape by pruning. It withstands considerable frost and usually sprouts in spring even when frosted back.

**Use good tools** All gardeners need a strong spade and fork, sharp secateurs and long-handled loppers, a hand trowel, fork and weeder, and a wheelbarrow. A 'ladies' spade and fork are very useful as well. Keep your tools clean and rust-free.

## Metarungia longistrobus

### Metarungia

**Size:** 1–3 x 1–2 m (wild), up to 2 x 1 m (garden)
**Natural habitat:** *Metarungia* is restricted to a few localities in eastern Mpumalanga, where it is found on rocky hills.
**Growth form:** It is an upright evergreen shrub with fairly dense foliage. New leaves are bluish with a silvery sheen. The blue colour is retained for several months before leaves adopt their mid-green mature colour. Both leaf colours are present at any one time. The pale orange flowers are arranged in vertical spikes with overlapping bracts, conveying the impression of a shrimp plant. The fruits are dry when mature and click audibly as they release their seeds.
**Propagation:** Seed.
**Uses:** *Metarungia* makes a wonderful garden plant in a hot dry spot. Do not be put off by its miserable appearance in a pot in a nursery. A seedling grows to full size within two years, flowering in its first year. A mature plant flowers all summer and well into autumn. Sunbirds and butterflies enjoy the flowers. Once flowering is over, the friendly click of dispersing seeds is a feature of many a warm dry winter afternoon. Self-sown seed germinates readily and a small thicket results after three or four years. *Metarungia* enjoys moderate rainfall and a warm summer.

## Mitriostigma axillare

### Small false loquat

**Size:** 1–3 x 1–3 m (wild), up to 2 x 3 m (garden)
**Natural habitat:** *Mitriostigma* is indigenous to the KwaZulu-Natal coast and to the eastern Escarpment, where it is confined to the shade of coastal, dune and mist-belt forests.
**Growth form:** It is a dense rounded shrub. The leaves are glossy with a waxy texture. On the undersurface the veins are prominent and bright pink. All growing points too, are pink. The flowers are pretty, white, with the entrance to the corolla rolled back like a trumpet. Their scent is said to be the sweetest of any indigenous flower. Flowering peaks in spring but continues on and off all summer. The fruits are spherical and orange.
**Propagation:** Seed.
**Uses:** *Mitriostigma* is a wonderful foliage and flowering specimen. This shrub can be grown in the shade but revels in full sunshine where leaf colours intensify and flowering is more profuse. Growth rate is modest – about 40 cm per year – but first flowering occurs in the second year. Fruiting has not so far been seen outside the natural range. Because it never gets large, *Mitriostigma* can be grown in the smallest garden and is well worth a prime spot. It likes moderate to good rainfall and a warm summer.

**Rooted cuttings** Many shrubs can be propagated by means of 'layering'. Pin a low branch onto the ground with a heavy stone and once roots have formed, treat it as a rooted cutting. (Treatment of cuttings is explained in more detail on pages 5 and 6 of the Introduction.)

## Monanthotaxis caffra

### Dwaba-berry

**Size:** 2–4 x 1–2 m (wild), up to 3 x 2 m (garden)
**Natural habitat:** This species is found naturally in a broad coastal strip from the Eastern Cape northwards. It occurs in evergreen forests, usually in the shady interior.
**Growth form:** *Monanthotaxis* is a low sprawling shrub that becomes a small scrambler given some light. The twigs are a beautiful copper. The side branches hug a host trunk so that *Monanthotaxis* appears to be climbing up a ladder. It has exceptionally beautiful foliage, the leaves being dark green above and quite a bright blue below. The fruits are also pretty, reddish-orange with a waxy finish. This plant is host to a variety of butterflies.
**Propagation:** Seed. *Monanthotaxis* must be planted out quickly to avoid root-cramping.
**Uses:** *Monanthotaxis* is best grown against a support, a trellis being ideal. Fruit is first produced at about two years within the natural range, at four years outside it. Once planted out, growth is rapid, individual shoots growing 2 m or so per year. Like many forest undergrowth plants, *Monanthotaxis* grows much better in cultivation than in the wild. Being small and fire-sensitive, it is restricted to the protection of shady forest trees. It only realises its full potential in sunny gardens.

## Mondia whitei

### Mondia

**Size:** 3–12 m long (wild), up to 8 m long (garden)
**Natural habitat:** *Mondia* grows naturally on the north coast of KwaZulu-Natal, and is common in swamp and riverine forest.
**Growth form:** It is a vigorous creeper, capable of scaling the forest canopy, but never develops a thick woody stem. Its main climbing aids are downward-pointing comb-like structures that encircle the stems at the base of every leaf. The leaves are large and heart-shaped, the perfect foil for the remarkable flowers, which are bicoloured stars, maroon framing green, and borne in tight bunches in early summer. The fruits, almost as interesting, resemble pairs of blunt ox-horns and are conspicuous in mid-winter when the foliage thins out. They split to release fluffy seeds.
**Propagation:** Seed.
**Uses:** *Mondia* is best planted along a fence where its Jack-and-the-Beanstalk qualities can be given full rein. *Mondia* is a 'twiner', as opposed to a rambler; new shoots do not grow into space but knit back into the fence. After two years, a 15 m length of fence will be covered and flowering begins then. *Mondia* must have a warm summer and prefers good rainfall or a high water table. However, the shrub grows well enough in moderate rainfall.

**Seasonal secrets** Although autumn colours are beautiful, they are quite functional. When the plant's water supply is reduced by the onset of drought or frost, it prepares to discard the leaves. The green chlorophyll is retrieved from the leaves by the plant, and coloured waste metabolic products in the leaves have their brief moment of glory.

## Mundulea sericea

### Cork bush

**Size:** 2–3 x 2–3 m (wild), up to 2.5 x 2 m (garden)
**Natural habitat:** *Mundulea* occurs in Zululand and over much of the northeast. It is found in all sorts of habitats – from the sandy grasslands around St Lucia to dry woodland, koppies and even deeply eroded dongas.
**Growth form:** It is a small shrubby tree. The bark is very thick and corky and deeply fissured. The leaves are an unusual pale silvery bluish-green that gleams in the sunshine. *Mundulea* is more or less evergreen. The flowers are outstanding, pea-shaped and a delicate lilac, cascading in sprays. Occasional plants have white flowers. Once the flowers are finished, bunches of pods persist for several months.
**Propagation:** Seed.
**Uses:** *Mundulea* can be recommended as a good flowering specimen, especially since it has an extended flowering period and sometimes flowers twice in one summer. It is a must for gardeners who crave grey or blue foliage and would make an unusual hedge. Growth rate varies greatly with climate. In a garden within its natural range, a chunky bush 2 m tall and heavily laden with pods resulted after two years. In an area that experiences high rainfall and moderate frost, eight years were required to achieve the same effect.

## Myrsine africana

### Cape myrtle

**Size:** 1–3 x 1–2.5 m (wild), up to 1.5 x 1 m (garden)
**Natural habitat:** *Myrsine* is found naturally in the cool, wet parts of South Africa, ranging from the Western Cape to the KwaZulu-Natal uplands, the central Highveld and eastern Escarpment. It occurs on the edge of forest and among rocks.
**Growth form:** *Myrsine* is typically shrubby, upright and slim. The leaves are tiny, glossy and delicately serrated. Bursts of red new growth flush throughout spring and summer. Young twigs are always a rich purple. The flowers are small but very pretty, the stamens protruding to create pink bottlebrushes. The fruits are berries, initially pink but deep purple when mature, and are eaten by birds.
**Propagation:** Seed, but germination is sporadic.
**Uses:** *Myrsine* is one of the prettiest of all shrubs and could be used as a specimen in a tiny garden or as a fringe on the sunny side of a forest clump. It would also be ideal for a steep rockery in high rainfall areas or, if closely planted, would make a miniature screen. Flowering begins at about four years within the natural range. Rate of growth is moderate – about 40 cm per year. *Myrsine* thrives in hot or cold areas provided that rainfall is high; it also enjoys cold and temperate areas with moderate rainfall.

**Spring leaf colours** The phenomenon of red, brown, blue or white spring leaves is the result of the different rates of production of various pigments. If the green chlorophyll is produced last, we enjoy the other colours while they are still visible, and before they are obscured by the intensity of the green.

## Ochna natalitia

**Natal plane, Coast boxwood**

**Size:** 3–6 x 2–5 m (wild), up to 4 x 3 m (garden)
**Natural habitat:** *O. natalitia* is found in much of the south and east. This shrub occurs among rocks in grassland and on evergreen forest edges.
**Growth form:** It is an erect shrub. *O. natalitia* is noted for its foliage. It has finely serrate glossy leaves with embossed parallel veins. There may be a short deciduous period towards the end of winter. New spring growth is metallic purple, turning red and finally green. *O. natalitia* flowers with great gusto and reliability in spring. The yellow flowers are about 2 cm in diameter, with wavy petals. They make a brilliant contrast with the red leaves. The fruit consists of black berry-like structures attached to the swollen red sepals, so that it resembles Mickey Mouse's face. Birds eat the fruits.
**Propagation:** Seed germinates readily but must be very fresh; viability is lost about three days after picking.
**Uses:** *O. natalitia* is worth prime place. Growth speed is about 50 cm per year and flowering begins in the second year. *O. natalitia* also makes a good screen which will not grow too tall. It grows best where the summer is warm and rainfall high but enjoys most climates. It withstands moderate drought.

## Ochna serrulata

**Carnival bush**

**Size:** 1–3 x 1–3 m (wild), up to 2 x 2 m (garden)
**Natural habitat:** *O. serrulata* is found naturally in much of the south and east and is common in places. It occurs among rocks in grassland.
**Growth form:** It is usually an erect shrub. It is noted for its foliage. It has tiny, finely serrate, glossy leaves with embossed parallel veins. New spring growth is metallic purple, turning red and finally green. *O. serrulata* flowers in early spring. The flowers are yellow and about 2 cm in diameter, with wavy petals. They cover the plant, making a brilliant contrast with the red leaves. The fruit consists of black berry-like structures attached to the swollen red sepals, so that it resembles Mickey Mouse's face. Birds eat the fruits.
**Propagation:** Seed germinates readily but must be very fresh; viability is lost about three days after picking.
**Uses:** *O. serrulata* is worth prime place, especially in a tiny garden. Growth speed is about 30 cm per year and flowering begins in the second year. It prefers full sunshine but performs well in partial shade too. It grows best where the summer is warm and rainfall high but enjoys most climates. This shrub withstands moderate drought and is easily protected from frost against a north-facing wall.

**Hairy leaves** Leaf hairs reduce the speed of wind over the leaf surface and help to reduce water transpiration. These flattened hairs also reflect light and cause the leaves to shimmer grey or silver when the sun shines on wind-blown leaves.

## Ormocarpum trichocarpum

**Caterpillar bush**

**Size:** 2–3 x 2–3 m (wild), up to 2 x 2 m (garden)
**Natural habitat:** *Ormocarpum* is confined to the warmer parts of the north and east, where it occurs in dry woodland. It is equally at home on hot rocky hillsides or on clay flats.
**Growth form:** It is a small stiff shrub or tree; in the wild it always has a craggy shape. The very thick corky bark is fissured and one of the most striking examples of this form of fire defence. The leaves are compound and finely divided. The canopy is small and sparse, casting virtually no shade. *Ormocarpum* has both lovely flowers and unique fruits. The flowers are purple and pea-like, with conspicuous veins, and borne in late summer. The fruits are pods covered with stiff golden-brown hairs, making them resemble caterpillars.
**Propagation:** Seed.
**Uses:** *Ormocarpum* is ideal for a small sunny garden because it takes up virtually no space and does not interfere with anything else. It makes a lovely flowering specimen and fruits outside the natural range. A two-year-old plant, not yet 1 m tall, has already flowered and the corky bark is developing. *Ormocarpum* enjoys a warm summer with moderate rainfall. It has yet to be tested in frost.

## Oxyanthus pyriformis

**Natal loquat**

**Size:** 3–8 x 3–7 m (wild), up to 6 x 5 m (garden)
**Natural habitat:** This species is confined to the KwaZulu-Natal coast where it is common in the forest undergrowth.
**Growth form:** It is usually single-stemmed but branches low down, forming a thickset mass. Although generally poor of form, this shrub does has superb foliage and is tropically extravagant, the leaves being large and beautifully veined. The flowers are works of art, white and showy. The spiky corolla tubes are 8 cm long, very thin and held vertically. Individual flowers are tightly bunched so that the corollas are massed in parallel. The fruits are yellow or orange, soft and also quite large.
**Propagation:** Seed.
**Uses:** *O. pyriformis* is worth a prime place as a flowering and foliage specimen. Flowering begins at four years. Fruiting does not seem to occur outside the natural range. Specimens cultivated in the open often develop a neat pyramidal shape, with dense branching at ground level. This makes it a useful screening plant. *O. pyriformis* will thrive given a warm wet summer and a frost-free winter. In the wild it often lives in full shade but in the garden it prefers light shade or full sun.

**Pollination** White flowers are pollinated by insects, which generally have poor eyesight but a good sense of smell, so nearly all white flowers are scented. Nocturnal white flowers tend to be more strongly scented – because they are, obviously, harder to see in the darkness – and are often pollinated by moths.

## Pachypodium saundersii

**Kudu lily**

**Size:** 1–1.5 x 1–1.5 m (wild), up to 1 x 1 m (garden)
**Natural habitat:** It is a lowveld inhabitant, usually occurring in sunny spots on hot rocky hillsides.
**Growth form:** This is a fat succulent with silvery-grey bark and a trunk sometimes thicker than it is tall. It has a few stubby branches covered in long, sharp spines. The leaves are beautiful, stiffly erect, and very glossy. The leafless period may last six months. In early winter *Pachypodium* produces lovely white flowers with frilly petals. Despite their delicate appearance, these are quite long-lasting. They are followed by fruits resembling thin pairs of ox-horns. They split lengthways when mature, releasing wind-dispersed seeds.
**Propagation:** Seed.
**Uses:** *Pachypodium* is an exciting, almost bizarre accent plant. It is ideal for a north-facing rockery, provided that it never gets shaded, as this suppresses flowering. It grows in a virtually waterless environment and needs watering only when the trunk starts shrinking; it can easily be over-watered. It grows well in a tub, which can be half-sheltered under an overhanging patio roof in high rainfall areas. *Pachypodium* needs a warm summer and frost-free winter. In a marginal climate site it close to a north-facing wall.

## Pavetta gardeniifolia

**Common bride's bush**

**Size:** 2–5 x 2–5 m (wild), up to 3 x 3 m (garden)
**Natural habitat:** This species occurs throughout most of the east of South Africa. It is usually found on rocky outcrops.
**Growth form:** *P. gardeniifolia* is a stiff craggy little tree, or more often a multi-stemmed shrub. It is deciduous in a dry winter. The leaves bear bacterial nodules, which appear as regularly spaced black dots or streaks. These enhance the beauty of the foliage and represent an interesting example of symbiosis, the bacterium enjoying a secure home while transforming atmospheric nitrogen into a form the plant can use. The flowers are white, vivid yet delicate, sweetly scented and produced in such masses as to cover the plant. They are followed by a profusion of small black berries greatly enjoyed by birds.
**Propagation:** Seed, and reasonably easily from cuttings.
**Uses:** *P. gardeniifolia* can be grown as a pride-of-place specimen, or in a shrubbery or dry rockery, and is ideal for a bird garden. Its drought-hardiness and interesting shape make it a successful container plant. First flowering occurs at about three years but fruiting has not been observed outside the natural range. Speed of growth is about 40 cm per year.

**Quid pro quo** *Pavetta* leaves have bacterial nodules, appearing as black dots or streaks on both sides of the leaves. This is an interesting example of symbiosis – the bacterium enjoys a secure home and, in turn, benefits the plant by transforming nitrogen in the atmosphere into a form the plant can use.

## Pavetta lanceolata

**Forest bride's bush**

**Size:** 2–3 x 3–4 m (wild), up to 3 x 3 m (garden)
**Natural habitat:** This is the most common and widespread *Pavetta*, occurring throughout much of the east of the country. It grows on the fringes of evergreen forest and among scrub on rocky outcrops.
**Growth form:** It is usually shrubby, the foliage dense. The leaves are thin and pointed and very glossy. They bear the typical *Pavetta* bacterial nodules, which appear as regularly spaced black dots or streaks. However, these are not as obvious as in *P. gardeniifolia*. The masses of delicate white flowers are sweetly scented and cover the plant. The common name derives from the confetti effect of flowering. The fruit is a small black berry liked by birds.
**Propagation:** Seed, and reasonably easily from cuttings.
**Uses:** *P. lanceolata* can be grown as a pride-of-place specimen or as part of a shrubbery or screen, and is ideal for a bird garden, even when space is limited. It grows about 40 cm per year. Flowering begins in midsummer and may extend into autumn. First flowering occurs at about three years. *P. lanceolata* enjoys almost any climate except that with a hot dry summer.

## Pavetta revoluta

**Dune bride's bush**

**Size:** 3–5 x 3–4 m (wild), up to 3 x 3 m (garden)
**Natural habitat:** *P. revoluta* is confined to the coasts of the southeast where it is found in dune forest and dense scrub.
**Growth form:** It tends to be shrubby but may be single-stemmed and grow as an upright tree, even when small. The leaves are thick and leathery. They bear the typical *Pavetta* bacterial nodules, which appear as regularly spaced black dots or streaks. The sweetly scented white flowers are vivid yet delicate and produced in such masses as to cover the plant. The fruit is a small black berry, decorated by a persistent calyx and borne in tight bunches. Birds love the fruits.
**Propagation:** Seed, and reasonably easily from cuttings.
**Uses:** *P. revoluta* can be grown as a pride-of-place specimen or as part of a shrubbery, and is ideal for a bird garden even when space is limited. It is especially useful in a beach garden. Flowering takes place in spring and first flowering occurs at about three years. It is slow-growing, with maximum rate being about 30 cm per year. *P. revoluta* likes a warm summer with moderate to high rainfall. Frost tolerance is unknown.

**Natural growth** Don't plant shrubs too close to a wall. Their natural all-round growth will force the plants to grow away from the wall at an unnatural angle. Leave enough space behind the shrubs for them to grow naturally.

## Phyllanthus reticulatus

**Potato bush**

**Size:** 2–10 x 2–6 m (wild), up to 7 x 5 m (garden)
**Natural habitat:** This species is found in the eastern lowlands. It occurs in deciduous woodland, often in thickets and on termite mounds.
**Growth form:** This shrub tends to scramble, even though older specimens have a substantial trunk. Within a bush clump, long slender branches up to 8 m long protrude in all directions. As its name suggests, *Phyllanthus* is responsible for the strong smell of baked potatoes characteristic of a hot, late afternoon in the Lowveld. The smell is caused by flowers so tiny they are almost invisible. The flowers are followed by a prolific crop of black berries, relished by birds.
**Propagation:** Seed.
**Uses:** *Phyllanthus* can hardly be described as beautiful but is a must for those who love the smell of the Lowveld. Flowering commences at two years and the flowering period is long, if irregular: up to eight months in total during the year. The potato smell is strong and carries up to 200 m. The untidy shape is best used in a bush clump or to fill an unruly corner. Growth is rampant and a mound 3 m high and 5 m in diameter forms after three years. *Phyllanthus* likes a warm climate.

## Plectranthus ecklonii

**Large spur-flower**

**Size:** 1–2.5 m x 0.5–1.5 m (wild), up to 2 x 1 m (garden)
**Natural habitat:** This species is common in the warmer, damper parts of the south and southeast. It nearly always forms soft thickets in forest undergrowth.
**Growth form:** *Plectranthus* is a soft-wooded slim upright perennial. It belongs to the mint family and crushed leaves have a distinct smell. The flowers are mauve tubes, borne in erect spikes. Variants with pink, purple or white flowers are known. The flowering peak occurs in autumn.
**Propagation:** Cuttings, which ensure preservation of a desired flower colour. They root best in river sand. Roots appear within 10 to 14 days and the cuttings are then ready to plant out.
**Uses:** *Plectranthus* will grow in full sun in cooler areas. However, its great value is in filling huge bare spots that are a feature of an over-mature garden dominated by shade. Note that not all shaded positions are equal. Some trees, like the jacaranda, poison everything beneath the canopy with leaf secretions. *Plectranthus* needs a dormant period in winter after flowering; prune out old stems and encourage new shoots. *Plectranthus* grows to full size and is covered with flowers in its first year. It cannot stand drought, but evades most frost in shaded positions.

**Shades of yellow** The yellow colour in flowers is due to a pigment called xanthophyll; deeper shades, verging on orange, are caused by the carotene pigment. Flowers often have darker markings, pointing the way to their pollen for bees, which are the main pollinators of the insect world.

## Plectroniella armata

**False turkey-berry**

**Size:** 4–6 x 4–6 m (wild), up to 4 x 4 m (garden)
**Natural habitat:** *Plectroniella* is widespread in the warmer parts of the east and north. It occurs in deciduous woodland where it is often a component of impenetrable thickets.
**Growth form:** *Plectroniella* is usually shrubby but may grow into an upright tree. It has a markedly right-angled branching pattern and powerful spines. Plectroniella is deciduous, displaying its formidable spine pattern to best advantage in winter. The flowers are white and showy, with a sweet scent. The orange fleshy fruits are produced in bunches. They are very sweet as they turn brown and make a good jelly.
**Propagation:** Seed.
**Uses:** *Plectroniella* is worth growing for its flowers and fruits, although fruiting has not yet been seen outside the natural range. It also makes an interesting form specimen, growing straight, slim and neat in the absence of browsing animals, or can be placed on the edge of a screen or bush clump. Its thorns also make it useful as a barrier plant. First flowering occurs at four years. Growth is reasonably fast, about 70 cm per year. Frost tolerance is unknown.

## Plumbago auriculata

**Plumbago**

**Size:** 2–5 m long (wild), up to 4 m long (garden)
**Natural habitat:** *Plumbago* is common in the Eastern Cape and KwaZulu-Natal, more localised further north. It is usually found in thick deciduous woodland.
**Growth form:** It is a modest scrambler and weaves its way through small trees, spilling trailing branches from the edge of the canopy. It is evergreen but thins in a dry winter. *Plumbago* is noted for its flowers, which are a cheerful pale blue. They are borne almost all year round and are profuse in summer.
**Propagation:** Usually propagated from suckers or cuttings.
**Uses:** It can be planted against a fence and will cover a 6 m span after about four years. *Plumbago* also grows well if planted next to supporting plants. It never overwhelms its support and looks particularly attractive if mixed with *Tecomaria* or *Acacia karroo*. Without support it tends to flop over and needs to spill down a bank. Flowering begins at one year. *Plumbago* grows best if the summer is warm and rainfall moderate to good but survives almost anything except severe frost and drought. A closely related species, *P. zeylonica*, has white flowers but otherwise resembles *P. auriculata*, and can be used in the same way.

**The reason it's blue** Anthocyanin pigments cause the blue colour in flowers that have alkaline cell sap. Blue flowers are pollinated primarily by bees, which are able to see ultraviolet light that the human eye cannot detect.

## Podranea ricasoliana

**Port St John's creeper**

**Size:** 6–18 m long (wild), up to 15 m long (garden)
**Natural habitat:** This plant comes from the coastal forests of the Eastern Cape.
**Growth form:** It is a rampant woody creeper, most evident when flowering fronds spill out of the forest canopy. *Podranea* has attractive divided leaves but its flowers are the most striking feature. These are present in profusion almost throughout the year. They are large pink-and-white trumpets with streaking in the throat, maturing in sequence on any one branch. The fruit is a dry pod.
**Propagation:** Seed, but more usually from a branch that has touched the ground and rooted. Pinning hanging branches to the ground with a brick will enable them to root there. These branches can be cut either side of the rooted section and then transplanted.
**Uses:** *Podranea* is suitable only for a fairly large garden or a long stretch of bare fence. Flowering begins in the first year and, being evergreen, *Podranea* makes a complete screen. Growth rate is often 3 m per year, even 5 m under ideal conditions. Indeed it is almost too vigorous and damaged roots may send up suckers all over the place. This creeper grows best in a warm climate with good rainfall but tolerates some frost and moderate rainfall.

## Polygala myrtifolia

**September bush**

**Size:** 2–3 x 2–3 m (wild), up to 2.5 x 2.5 m (garden)
**Natural habitat:** It occurs naturally from the Western Cape to KwaZulu-Natal, always in areas of good rainfall. It grows in most habitats except the interior of evergreen forests and may be prominent on the seaward edge of dune forest.
**Growth form:** *P. myrtifolia* is a rounded shrub. Its leaves are small, the foliage soft. It is noted for its flowering displays. Flowers are pale purple to pink, individual flowers exhibiting a range of shades and being conspicuously veined. Flowering is almost continuous. Large, brightly coloured carpenter bees are attracted to the flowers and they drill holes and nest in any dead wood nearby.
**Propagation:** Seed. In the garden, this shrub often produces seedings around its base, which can be harvested.
**Uses:** *P. myrtifolia* is the most reliable of all flowering shrubs. First flowering occurs in the second year. It can be used on the outer fringes of a sunny shrubbery but looks its best placed beside water. The foliage provides an adequate screen for much of the year. *P. myrtifolia* is especially useful in beachfront gardens. Initial growth is fast, about 1 m per year. Subsequently, the plant thickens out. It likes a warm or temperate climate with at least moderate rainfall.

**Shrubs for coastal gardens** Sterile sand near the beach supports only the few shrubs that can stand the wind and over-efficient drainage. Most rewarding are *Allophylus natalensis, Eugenia capensis* and *Polygala myrtifolia.*

## Polygala virgata

### Bloukappies

**Size:** 1–3 x 1–2 m (wild), up to 2 x 1 m (garden)
**Natural habitat:** *P. virgata* occurs in the cool damp uplands, ranging from the southwestern Cape to the east and north of South Africa. It is nearly always found on stream banks.
**Growth form:** It is a spindly shrub with sparse foliage. *P. virgata* is noted for its flowering displays. The flowers are pale purple to pink, individual flowers exhibiting a range of shades and being conspicuously veined. The flowering period lasts six months or more. The flowers are evenly spaced, hanging in rows along almost leafless twigs. The beauty of this arrangement is accentuated by the otherwise scraggly physique of this plant.
**Propagation:** Seed.
**Uses:** *P. virgata* can be used as a flowering specimen but must be clumped for effect. It looks its best when placed beside water. First flowering occurs in the second year. Initial growth is fast, about 1 m per year. Subsequently vertical growth slows as the plant thickens out and it matures at about three years. *P. virgata* is fairly short-lived; the trick is to leave some self-seeded offspring to take over as the original plant fades away. It dislikes drought but withstands considerable frost.

## Protea eximia

### Broad-leaved protea

**Size:** 2–5 x 2–5 m (wild), up to 4 x 6 m (garden)
**Natural habitat:** This shrub is widespread in the fynbos of the southern Cape mountains, occurring over a wide range of altitude and climate.
**Growth form:** It is a robust bush or squat tree, branching from the base. The leaves are bluish, furry when young and contrast nicely with the red twigs. Flowering performance is about the best of all proteas. Flowering heads are large, predominantly red, tipped black. They are visited by brightly coloured beetles and are a favourite of sugarbirds which also often nest in *P. eximia*. Flowering may last nearly all year.
**Propagation:** Seed, after a warm soaking; and cuttings, best taken in November.
**Uses:** *P. eximia* makes a wonderful flowering specimen and a prime focus in a bird garden, even outside the natural range. Indeed, it grows best in the summer rainfall of KwaZulu-Natal. Flowering begins at three years and *P. eximia* may live 20 years or more. Heavy pruning, especially in the first 2–4 years, greatly boosts the number of flowering shoots and prevents the plant getting too tall. Flowers are best picked when the unopened bud becomes soft-tipped. *P. eximia* is a commercial cut flower proposition and makes the best hybrids.

**Flower arrangements** Add local flavour to your next arrangement by using *Alberta magna*, *Burchellia bubalina*, *Leonotis leonurus*, *Ochna serrulata* or *Polygala virgata*. For beautiful foliage try *Mackaya bella* (the flowers are good too) and *Carissa* species.

## Protea repens

### Sugarbush

**Size:** 2–4.5 x 2–4.5 m (wild), up to 4 x 6 m (garden)
**Natural habitat:** *P. repens* occurs virtually throughout the winter rainfall region. It is usually found at the base or on the lower slopes of mountains, often in large colonies.
**Growth form:** It is an upright bush, sometimes tree-like. The flowering heads are large and very beautiful. The colour varies regionally. Brightest reds come from the Eastern Cape, summer being the flowering season. Further west the flowers may be cream, pink or two-tone, usually appearing in autumn or winter. Sunbirds love them all. This species produces by far the most nectar of all proteas (the nectar actually overflowing sometimes), hence its common name.
**Propagation:** Seed, after a warm soaking; and cuttings, best taken in November.
**Uses:** This is the most adaptable of all proteas, essential in a bird garden. It grows as well in clay as in sand, and particularly well in the summer rainfall region. Flowering begins at three years. Performance is improved by repeated pruning when the plant is 2–4 years old. Growth rate is about 30 cm per year and *P. repens* may live to be 20 or more. It must have good rainfall and regular breezes. Make a rustic sugar from *P. repens*'s nectar, by concentrating it, as early settlers did.

## Psoralea pinnata

### Fountain bush

**Size:** 1–4 x 1–3 m (wild), up to 3 x 2 m (garden)
**Natural habitat:** *Psoralea* occurs from the southwestern Cape, through KwaZulu-Natal to the eastern Escarpment. It is always found in damp habitats beside streams or vleis, lush grassland or on forest edges, both at the coast and inland.
**Growth form:** This shrub is bright and evergreen, with exquisitely delicate foliage similar to that of the tamarisk. The leaves are divided into needle-like leaflets and release a scent when crushed. *Psoralea* bears masses of light-blue pea-shaped flowers, although some plants have dark-blue flowers and others may have almost white flowers. Flowering begins in midsummer and may last six months.
**Propagation:** Seed.
**Uses:** The foliage is dense enough to make an adequate screen. Flowering begins at two years. *Psoralea* is close to that dream plant so often requested: something that grows almost instantly to full size, without getting too big, always looks nice and doesn't make a mess. In a suitable climate – warm temperate, and with good rainfall – *Psoralea* grows at least 1 m per year initially, slowing down as it thickens out. The shrub has yet to be tested in extreme conditions, but is unlikely to tolerate drought.

**Propagating proteas** Seeds of the *Protea* family benefit from a 'warm soak' treatment: put them in water at 50 °C for half an hour before planting.

## Psychotria capensis

**Cream psychotria, Izele**

**Size:** 3–5 x 3–5 m (wild), up to 3 x 3 m (garden)
**Natural habitat:** *Psychotria* is found naturally in the southern Cape, much of KwaZulu-Natal and the eastern Escarpment. It is usually found in the undergrowth of evergreen forest, less often among rocks in grassland.
**Growth form:** It is a small tree, often shrubby. The foliage has a tropical look, the leaves being dark green, thick and glossy. The bright yellow flowers, although small, are produced in conspicuous bunches. The fruits are brightly coloured berries, at first green, then turning yellow, red and black, all colours being present in a single bunch. This is an obvious adaptation to retain the attention of birds over an extended period, and it succeeds in doing so.
**Propagation:** Seed.
**Uses:** *Psychotria* is ideal as a solo specimen, for a flowering screen and as part of a bird garden. It could also be used as a thicket to fill a damp spot in fairly dense shade. Flowering commences at two years. Although largely restricted to the shade in the wild, *Psychotria* grows well in full sunshine, provided that rainfall is moderate to high. When rainfall is marginal it does better in light shade. Psychotria grows about 50 cm per year. It cannot tolerate drought or frost.

## Psydrax locuples

**Krantz quar**

**Size:** 2–4 x 2–4 m (wild), up to 3 x 3 m (garden)
**Natural habitat:** *Psydrax* is restricted to the eastern Lowveld and the warmer parts of KwaZulu-Natal. It occurs in coastal forest and among rocks in grassland.
**Growth form:** It is usually a small shrub, but when not nibbled or burnt can develop into a little tree. It has a striking branching pattern. Branches grow in opposite pairs exactly at right angles to the parent branch. These pairs will in turn be at right angles in the third dimension to adjacent pairs of branches. The final product has a 'computer-built' appearance. The leaves are small and glossy, with wavy margins, so reflect light from all angles. The flowers are small and white, but produced in profusion, with all the flowers maturing simultaneously, creating a fine show. The fruits are lopsided black shiny berries. They are an important food for birds.
**Propagation:** Seed.
**Uses:** *Psydrax* is worth its place for the beauty of its foliage and flowers. Another attraction is its value to birds. It is also an ideal component for bush clumps or screens. Growth rate is about 40 cm per year. It tolerates a little frost but grows best in a warm environment with moderate to good rainfall.

**Shade and shrubs** Most shrubs prefer sunshine. Once they become shaded, they may grow at only a tenth of the expected rate and refuse to flower. A few shrubs actually prefer shade, though. Use *Andrachne* and *Englerodaphne* for deep shade, and *Psychotria* and *Mackaya* for partial shade.

## Putterlickia verrucosa

### False forest spike-thorn

**Size:** 1–4 x 1–4 m (wild), up to 3 x 3 m (garden)
**Natural habitat:** *Putterlickia* is restricted to a broad coastal belt from the Eastern Cape northwards and from here inland up along hot low-lying valleys. It occurs in dune forest, on the edges of other forest types and in woodland.
**Growth form:** It is a rambling shrub, even when single-stemmed. It has very long, sharp spines and the bark of young branches is covered with white spots. The leaves are glossy and clustered in little bunches. This arrangement maximises exposure of the distinctive bark and spines. The flowers are tiny stars, quite pretty, and followed by attractive fruits that resemble small balloons as they hang from long stalks. They mature to pink or orange, eventually splitting to reveal dark yellow seeds designed to tempt birds.
**Propagation:** Seed.
**Uses:** *Putterlickia* is pretty enough to be grown as a solo specimen or could be included in a smallish screen. The spines act as a perfect barrier. Fruiting has been noted at four years but not so far outside the natural range. Growth rate is about 50 cm per year. *Putterlickia* likes a warm climate, with at least moderate rainfall. It tolerates a little frost but is most useful in beach gardens.

## Rawsonia lucida

### Rawsonia

**Size:** 3–7 x 3–6 m (wild), up to 3 x 3 m (garden)
**Natural habitat:** *Rawsonia* is found naturally in a broad coastal strip in KwaZulu-Natal and to the wetter parts of the northeast. It is confined to the undergrowth of evergreen forest.
**Growth form:** *Rawsonia* is usually encountered as a shrub in fairly deep shade but becomes a small tree if it gets more light. On older plants the bark flakes, revealing rich chestnut patches. *Rawsonia* is evergreen and has outstanding foliage. The leaves are glossy dark-green, with a bold regular vein pattern and evenly spaced sharp teeth around the margin. The fruits are yellow spheres about 3 cm in diameter and make a nice display in late summer, whether draped on the tree or scattered beneath it.
**Propagation:** Seed.
**Uses:** *Rawsonia* is particularly useful because it thrives in semi-shade where its small size and beautiful foliage are a great asset. However, it grows perfectly well in full sun provided the climate is not too hot or dry. Fruiting begins at about four years and occurs outside the natural range. Growth is fairly slow, about 40 cm per year. *Rawsonia* grows best where the summer is warm and rainfall good. It is sensitive to frost but tolerates normal winter drought.

**How frost kills** Frost causes ice crystals to form inside plant cells, rupturing the cell membranes. Then, as ice forms, the remaining cell sap becomes concentrated, and vital proteins precipitate out. Either of these events can quickly kill the plant.

## Rhigozum obovatum

### Karoo pomegranate

**Size:** 1–3 x 1–3 m (wild), up to 2 x 2 m (garden)
**Natural habitat:** *R. obovatum* grows naturally in the Karoo and Eastern Cape, among rocks and in low-growing scrub.
**Growth form:** It is a rather scruffy little bush that is either multi-stemmed or branches low down. The branches bear fierce spines. The foliage is sparse and undistinguished but the flowers are gorgeous, bright, deep yellow, with a frilly texture, covering the tree in spring when it is leafless. The flowering display lasts for a week or two. The fruit is a small flat pod.
**Propagation:** Seed.
**Uses:** *R. obovatum* is worth growing not only for its flowers but for its interesting spine patterns and for its defensive value in a screen. Flowering begins after about four years. Best results are obtained if *R. obovatum* is planted in the hottest, most exposed spot in the garden. The north face of a rockery for succulents is ideal. It must never be watered or it will refuse to flower. Rate of growth is slow, about 30 cm per year, given a warm summer and moderate to low rainfall. *R. obovatum* withstands considerable frost and endures almost endless drought.

## Rhoicissus digitata

### Baboon grape

**Size:** 5–20 m long (wild), up to 15 m long (garden)
**Natural habitat:** *R. digitata* is found naturally in a broad coastal fringe from Cape Town to Zululand, then inland northwards. It occurs in most forest types, being especially common in dune forest and may be the sole coloniser of the windward side of the first dune.
**Growth form:** It is often a vigorous scrambler, with a woody rope-like trunk winding around anything in its quest for light. Sometimes this forms great coiled loops on the forest floor where it has outlived former supports. On coastal dunes, *R. digitata* needs nothing to climb but forms a twining mat. Only in these circumstances is new growth bright red. The grapes are black, quite large and can make a pleasant display.
**Propagation:** Seed.
**Uses:** *R. digitata* is a worker rather than a beauty. On a large pergola or if planted against a fence in full sun, it provides solid shelter and screening. At three years it will cover about a 15-m-span of fence and can be expected to be much larger than that at maturity. It is especially useful in a beach garden and to stabilise dunes on a large scale. It enjoys a warm or temperate climate with moderate to good rainfall, and tolerates slight frost.

**Quick cover with creepers** Ugly walls, fences and dead stumps can all be covered quite easily with creepers. For fast cover, and if there is plenty of space, use *Landolphia*, *Podranea* and *Rhoicissus*.

## Rhoicissus tomentosa

### Common forest grape

**Size:** 5–25 m long (wild), up to 15 m long (garden)
**Natural habitat:** *R. tomentosa* is found in evergreen forests in a broad coastal fringe from the southern Cape to Zululand and from there inland east and north.
**Growth form:** It is obviously related to the cultivated grape. It is a vigorous scrambler, with a woody rope-like trunk. Its bark is corky and wonderfully sculpted. The leaves are large, semicircular and elegantly veined. They are borne only where the plant emerges into the sun. New growth is covered with ginger hairs. The grapes are large and black and make a pleasant display. Birds eat them – and on a considerable scale judging by the number that germinate in gutters.
**Propagation:** Seed.
**Uses:** *R. tomentosa* is much more attractive than its stark performance in the wild suggests. If planted against a pergola or fence in full sun it remains densely leafy throughout the year and is altogether a fine foliage plant. The leading shoots bear pretty tendrils that anchor it firmly in place, providing a complete screen. At three years *R. tomentosa* covers about a 15-m-span of fence and can be expected to be much larger than that at maturity. It enjoys a warm climate with moderate to good rainfall.

## Rhus batophylla

### Steelpoort rhus

**Size:** 1–2 x 1–2 m (wild), up to 1.5 x 1 m (garden)
**Natural habitat:** *R. batophylla* is a very localised species, being confined in the wild to a small area near Steelpoort in the northeast, where it occurs in dry woodland.
**Growth form:** It is always small and shrubby, with a few erect stems. The leaves are exceptionally beautiful – blue-green above, white below – and markedly serrated. New growth points are furry white. The flowers are the prettiest of all *Rhus* species, being produced in pink masses. The tiny berries, too, are colourful and bright blood-red.
**Propagation:** Seed. If seed is not available, small cuttings will strike well enough.
**Uses:** This is a plant that fits into the smallest garden and is popular with foliage enthusiasts. It grows to its maximum height within four years, thickening a little thereafter. Flowering begins at three years but cannot be guaranteed: it seems that poor acid soils give best results but more research is needed to verify this. Because sexes are separate, it is essential that *R. batophylla* be planted in threes or more. Males cannot bear berries and nor will females if a source of pollen is too far away. It likes a warm summer but otherwise tolerates most climates.

**Not a *Rhus* by any name** *Rhus*, an attractive indigenous genus, has been given a bad name because it is often mistaken for the exotic '*Rhus*' – more properly named *Toxicodendron succedanea*. *Rhus* species all have leaves divided into three leaflets, and cause no allergic reactions, unlike *Toxicodendron succedanea*, which has many leaflets.

## Rhus burchellii

**Kuni bush**

**Size:** 3–5 x 3–5 m (wild), up to 3 x 3 m (garden)
**Natural habitat:** *R. burchellii* is widespread in the drier parts of the west and central interior of South Africa. It occurs in semi-desert scrub and on rocky hillsides.
**Growth form:** It tends to be shrubby, but younger plants often have a lovely branching pattern. Individual branches are perfectly candelabra-shaped and are arranged in a neat spiral on the parent branch. The foliage is another outstanding feature. The dark, shiny, green leaves are very small, with a clean-cut, crinkly shape. Some develop a waxy sheen. Fruits are tiny, red-brown and thin-fleshed; produced in cascades that attract small fruit-eating birds, notably white-eyes.
**Propagation:** Seed. If seed is not available, small cuttings strike well enough.
**Uses:** *R. burchellii* can be grown as a specimen and is ideal in a bird garden. Older plants retain most lower branches and foliage, even in a harsh climate, making an ideal screen or informal hedge. Flowering and fruiting usually begin in the second year. Growth rate is about 60 cm per year. *Rhus* has separate sexes. Males cannot bear berries and nor will females if a source of pollen is too far away. So plant *R. burchellii* in groups of three or greater numbers.

## Rhus crenata

**Dune crow-berry**

**Size:** 3–5 x 4–7 m (wild), up to 3 x 5 m (garden)
**Natural habitat:** This species of shrub grows naturally from the southwestern Cape to KwaZulu-Natal, occurring on coastal dunes. Single-species stands may form a thick, undulating carpet across the landscape.
**Growth form:** It is a dense and substantial shrub, with a spread up to twice its height. The lowest branches hug the ground. The leaves are neatly scalloped and glossy and bursts of new red growth appear throughout the year. The fruits are tiny bluish berries. Only female plants bear fruit.
**Propagation:** Seed. If seed is not available, use small cuttings.
**Uses:** *R. crenata* is worth growing for its foliage and makes a fine screen within three years. It is ideal in a bird garden. *R. crenata* is very useful in coastal gardens but grows equally well inland in a drier climate in shale. Initial growth rate is about 60 cm per year. It is important to remember that sexes are separate. Males cannot bear berries and nor will females if a source of pollen is too far away, so outside its natural range, *R. crenata* should be planted in threes or greater numbers. It likes a warm climate with at least moderate rainfall.

**A meeting point** Gardens are often the only place where people come into contact with birds and other wildlife. Plant flowering and fruiting shrubs that attract birds to your garden and they will provide you with many hours of enjoyment. (Shrubs with the bird symbol listed under their entry are ideal for this purpose.)

## Rhus dentata

**Nana berry**

**Size:** 2–4 x 3–5 m (wild), up to 3 x 4 m (garden)
**Natural habitat:** *R. dentata* is widespread but avoids the winter-rainfall and arid areas. It is particularly common in the mountains. It grows at the edges of evergreen forest, alongside streams and on rock outcrops in grassland.
**Growth form:** It can be single-stemmed and spreading, or shrubby. *R. dentata* has most attractive foliage; as the name suggests, the leaflets have large neat teeth. In autumn the leaves turn bronze, finally going brilliant red if the climate is cold enough. The flowers are tiny but produced in profusion and for a short period attract many insects and insectivorous birds such as warblers. Its tiny red-brown berries are produced in cascades, attracting small fruit-eating birds.
**Propagation:** Seed.
**Uses:** *R. dentata* can be grown as a specimen or in bush clumps and informal hedges. It is ideal in a bird garden. Flowering and fruiting begin in the second year. Note that sexes are separate. Males cannot bear berries and nor will females if a pollen source is too distant so plant at least three together. Growth rate is about 70 cm per year. *R. dentata* grows best where the summer is wet and the winter very cold. The red autumn colours do not develop in frost-free areas.

## Rhus discolor

**Grassveld currant**

**Size:** 0.5–1 x 0.5–1 m (wild), up to 1 x 1 m (garden)
**Natural habitat:** It is widespread in the damper grasslands of the east, from sea level to 2,000 m altitude. It occurs in thick grass, often in large numbers.
**Growth form:** It is an upswept shrub, nearly always multi-stemmed as a result of often being burnt back to ground level. The leaves are very handsome. The greyish-green of the upper surface contrasts strongly with the snow-white under-surface. The latter has a bold, raised vein pattern. Autumn sees a stunning colour change as the upper surface turns flaming red. The small shiny yellow-brown berries are borne in upright pyramids at branch tips. Only female plants bear fruit.
**Propagation:** Seed.
**Uses:** *R. discolor* is an outstanding foliage plant and pretty when in fruit. Because it is small, plant at least three to best show off autumn colours. The planting must be massed in the open where it will never be shaded. It grows to full size within two years. *R. discolor* does not need extra water during short droughts, and autumn colours tend to be suppressed by it. It grows best where there is a temperate summer with at least moderate rainfall. Cut straggly plants back to simulate fire and promote foliage production.

**Moving a shrub** If you find it necessary to move a shrub, water it well first, then dig out a good-sized root bole, and plant it with the same orientation in its new position as it had originally. Water it well again.

## Rhus glauca

### Blue kuni-bush

**Size:** 2–4 x 3–5 m (wild), up to 3 x 4 m (garden)
**Natural habitat:** This species occurs along the length of the southern Cape coast in dune scrub, where jackass penguins nest beneath it, and on other sandy soils. It extends inland in a few places to the Karoo fringes.
**Growth form:** It tends to be single-stemmed, branching low down, and usually wider than tall. The leaves are among the most handsome of all *Rhus*, distinctly bluish with clean-cut profile. The flowers are tiny but produced in profusion. The fruits are also tiny glossy red-brown berries produced in cascades that attract small birds.
**Propagation:** Seed. If seed is not available small cuttings can be used.
**Uses:** *R. glauca* is good-looking enough to make a specimen or can be grown in a bird garden, bush clump or informal hedge. It is especially useful at the coast where it enjoys the deep sand of beach gardens and screens off wind. Flowering and fruiting usually begin in the second year. Note that sexes are separate. Males cannot bear berries and neither will females if a pollen source is too distant, so plant three plants together. Growth rate is about 60 cm per year. It grows best in a warm summer, wet or dry.

## Rhus gueinzii

### Thorny karee

**Size:** 3–7 x 4–8 m (wild), up to 5 x 6 m (garden)
**Natural habitat:** *R. gueinzii* is confined to a coastal belt extending northwards from the Eastern Cape, and to the Lowveld. It occurs in dry woodland, often on termite mounds, and may form dense thickets. It also fringes forest clumps.
**Growth form:** Typically it is densely shrubby. The branches and smaller trunks bear large spines that eventually develop into branchlets. The leaflets are narrow and shiny. *R. gueinzii* is almost evergreen. In some winters it is never leafless, in others the deciduous period is brief. *R. gueinzii* produces lovely sprays of tiny, white flowers. It fruits regularly and profusely and the tree may be completely covered with bunches of red-brown berries.
**Propagation:** Seed.
**Uses:** *R. gueinzii* makes an interesting specimen and is ideal in a bush clump. It also makes a rather rambling, almost impenetrable hedge. Flowering and fruiting usually begin in the second year. In a bird garden it provides nest sites as well as food. Note that sexes are separate. Males cannot bear berries and neither will females if a pollen source is too distant. *R. gueinzii* grows 1 m or more per year. It grows best in a warm climate with at least moderate rainfall.

**The bat appetite** One bat eats 1,000 mosquitoes in an hour, so be kind to them if they are roosting in your roof. Better still – provide a bat-house especially for them. A rough-sawn box, 15 x 15 cm and 30 cm high, with a hinged, sloping roof and 2-cm slit in the bottom, is ideal. Fix it 2–3 m up a vertical tree trunk.

## Rhus krebsiana

### Matatiele rhus

**Size:** 2–3 x 2–3 m (wild), up to 2 x 2 m (garden)
**Natural habitat:** This has a restricted range, growing from the Eastern Cape to the southern Drakensberg foothills. It occurs at fairly high altitudes in patches of scrub forest.
**Growth form:** *R. krebsiana* is a stiff upright shrubby tree. The foliage is swept upwards. Young leaves are bright, glossy green, with an interesting colour change in midsummer when they prematurely turn 'autumn' shades of pastel pinks and oranges. Large bunches of small pinkish-brown fruits are produced at the same time. Only female plants bear fruit. The plant is leafless for a month or so before growing new leaves in late summer.
**Propagation:** Seed.
**Uses:** *R. krebsiana* makes an interesting foliage specimen with its summer colours. But note that the beautiful foliage changes seem to be suppressed if the plant receives extra water. It is useful for a bush clump or informal hedge in very cold areas and is ideal in a bird garden. Flowering and fruiting begin in the third year. Note that sexes are separate. Males cannot bear berries and neither will females if a pollen source is too distant. Plant at least three together. Growth is rapid – about 70 cm per year.

## Rhus nebulosa

### Sand taaibos

**Size:** 2–5 x 1–3 m (wild), up to 4 x 2 m (garden)
**Natural habitat:** *R. nebulosa* is confined to KwaZulu-Natal and the Eastern Cape where it is common in coastal lowland forest, especially fringing forest clumps.
**Growth form:** It is shrubby, with a tendency to scramble, sending out long shoots where the surrounding vegetation provides support. Flowering is exceptionally profuse, the end-product being storey upon storey of lacy pyramids. These flowers are by far the finest of all *Rhus*. The orange, slightly translucent fruits are produced in great quantities and at an early age, even in the first year, and outside the natural range and climate.
**Propagation:** Seed.
**Uses:** *R. nebulosa* will not make a tidy specimen and is best used in bush clumps, so that it can grow up through them and spill out from the top. If trained against a fence, it will cover a 4 m section in as many years. It is ideal for a bird garden. Note that sexes are separate. Males cannot bear berries and neither will females if a pollen source is too distant. *R. nebulosa* likes coastal conditions, growing best with warm summers and good rainfall. In frosty areas it is briefly deciduous and, remarkably, develops autumn colours.

**Know your plants** 'Indigenous' means homegrown, originating or produced naturally, in a specific place. Because conditions vary so much across South Africa, plants are typically indigenous to a particular area, not to the whole country. So, gardeners need to know exactly what region a plant comes from to find out if it is suitable for their garden too.

## Rhus tomentosa

**Wild currant**

**Size:** 2–4 x 2–4 m (wild), up to 3 x 3 m (garden)
**Natural habitat:** This species is found naturally in the cooler, wetter parts of the country, ranging from the Western Cape to the eastern Escarpment and Soutpansberg. It occurs on the edge of forests and especially among rocks.
**Growth form:** *R. tomentosa* is a small, densely shrubby tree. It has particularly attractive foliage; the deep green of the leaf upper surface with its clean-cut veins contrasts with the white undersurface. The tiny flowers are produced in sprays. They are followed by cascades of very small creamy berries.
**Propagation:** Seed. If seed is not available small cuttings of this shrub may be used.
**Uses:** *R. tomentosa* is quite pretty enough to be used as a specimen or makes a good screen since it remains evergreen even in a cold winter. It is ideal for a bird garden. Flowering and fruiting usually begin in the second year. Note that sexes are separate. Males cannot bear berries and neither will females if a source of pollen is too distant. Growth is fast – about 80 cm per year initially. After a year or two, vertical growth slows as the plant fills out. It can stand Johannesburg frost and an average winter drought. It probably would not enjoy a subtropical climate.

## Schotia afra

**Karoo boer-bean**

**Size:** 3–5 x 2–4 m (wild), up to 3 x 2 m (garden)
**Natural habitat:** This species has two populations, one in the Eastern Cape, the other in the Northern Cape. It occurs among low scrub and in deciduous thickets, being common in the Addo Elephant Park.
**Growth form:** *S. afra* has a variable growth habit. It can be a small tree, but is more commonly shrubby, even scrambling if part of a thicket. Alternatively, it gets cut right back by large herbivores. Its tiny leaflets give it a delicate air. Dark red bottlebrush flowers appear during summer. Flowering continues with variable intensity for up to six months. The flowers are not tubular but cup-shaped, so the generous supply of nectar is accessible to all birds, not just to sunbirds. The fruits are woody pods that turn from green to pink, before maturing to dark brown. This is the host plant of the butterfly *Deudorix antalis*.
**Propagation:** Seed, which germinates readily, even if it has been stored for some time.
**Uses:** *S. afra* is essential in a bird garden and is worth growing for the flowers alone. It is best used as a small specimen in a hot dry spot. First flowering can be expected at five years. Growth rate is about 30 cm per year. It thrives where summers are hot and rainfall low to moderate.

**Choosing the right path** If you want to create a path in your garden, choose between a single-file path and one that can accommodate more than one person. A disappearing single-file path makes your garden look longer, while the latter lets you walk around the garden with friends to enjoy the scenery.

## Schotia capitata

**Dwarf boer-bean**

**Size:** 3–6 x 2–4 m (wild), up to 4 x 3 m (garden)
**Natural habitat:** *S. capitata* occurs in Zululand and in the southern Lowveld of Mpumalanga. It grows in dry woodland, especially in hot, exposed positions and on termite mounds.
**Growth form:** It can be a neat small tree but it is usually shrubby, even scrambling in a thicket. In Umfolozi, *S. capitata* bowers are the favoured prey storage sites of leopards. Alternatively, *S. capitata* gets grazed down by black rhinos to form gleaming lawns. The handsome leaves are initially orange-brown, later turning a rich green. The flowers are dark red, with long bottlebrush stamens. They are borne during summer and the flowering period may last six months. The flowers are cup-shaped, so their generous supply of nectar is accessible to all birds, rather than just sunbirds. The flowers are followed by woody pods that disintegrate while still on the tree, revealing pale pink-and-yellow seeds.
**Propagation:** Seed, which may be stored for some time.
**Uses:** *S. capitata* is best used as a small specimen. It is ideal in a bird garden and is worth growing for the flowers alone. First flowering occurs at five years. Growth rate is about 50 cm per year. This shrub thrives where summers are hot and rainfall low to moderate.

## Scutia myrtina

**Cat-thorn, Droog-my-keel**

**Size:** 3–12 x 2–6 m (wild), up to 6 x 3 m (garden)
**Natural habitat:** *Scutia* is found in the evergreen forests of wetter regions – from the southwestern Cape to the far northeast, and from the coast to the highest forest patch in the Drakensberg.
**Growth form:** *Scutia* is usually shrubby, with a tendency to scramble if there is anything around to provide support. Some of the giant woody ropes that sprawl over the forest floor are *Scutia*. The leaves are glossy and attractive. The branches bear backward-curving spines that assist in clambering over neighbours. During winter, *Scutia* produces lots of small black berries with a bitter yet pleasant flavour. Birds like them.
**Propagation:** Seed.
**Uses:** *Scutia* is best used on a fence where its thorns and dense growth greatly improve the barrier. It is also useful in a mixed screen or forest patch in a bird garden. Fruiting begins at three years. Growth rate varies from over 1 m per year in a warm, wet climate with support, to about 30 cm per year in a cool climate without it. *Scutia* enjoys almost any climate, except one that is hot and dry, and is useful at the coast.

**Ensuring fruit** Some shrubs have separate male and female plants. Only fertilised females produce fruit, so grow at least two plants, to improve the chance of having both sexes, and, hence, of pollination. A young plant's sex cannot be told until it has flowered. Where fruit production matters try to choose a nursery plant that already has fruit.

## Senecio tamoides

**Canary creeper**

**Size:** 3–14 m long (wild), up to 9 m long (garden)
**Natural habitat:** This occurs naturally in the wetter parts of eastern South Africa. It is a creeper that grows on the edges of evergreen forest or dense scrub.
**Growth form:** Unlike most larger creepers it is not woody, but remains soft, almost succulent. The leaves are sculpted like ivy and have the texture of rubber. The flowers make a glorious display in early winter – bright yellow daisies that completely cover both the plant and its support. Butterflies of the Pieridae family visit them. As the flowers fade, they release dandelion-like seeds into passing breezes. *Senecio* may die back later in winter after heavy frost or prolonged drought.
**Propagation:** Seed, but cuttings are more convenient.
**Uses:** In a single season, climbing shoots grow 3–7 m given a suitable fence, pergola or dead tree. The dense foliage makes a screen or hides an ugly feature very quickly. Profuse flowering is guaranteed in the first season. It is therefore best to cut *Senecio* back, assuming that anything remains by early spring, to improve performance in the next cycle. *Senecio* likes high rainfall but tolerates a range of temperatures. Frost rarely kills this shrub, although severe early frost curtails flowering.

## Sesbania sesban

**River bean**

**Size:** 2–3 x 2–3 m (wild), up to 2.5 x 2 m (garden)
**Natural habitat:** *Sesbania* is restricted to the warmer parts of the east and southeast, being most common beside water, especially where seasonal flooding is usual. Typically, it is the first pioneer in areas stripped of vegetation.
**Growth form:** It may be shrubby or a soft, little tree. The foliage droops gracefully, tending to weep. *Sesbania* has pretty yellow pea-shaped flowers, the colour distinguishing it from its red-flowered alien invasive relative. Flowering continues on and off for most of the year. The fruits are long thin cylindrical pods that hang in masses like a miniature bamboo curtain. They rattle faintly in the wind.
**Propagation:** Seed.
**Uses:** *Sesbania* comes very close to the impatient novice gardener's dream of a plant that grows rapidly to a modest size and then stops, yet flowers throughout. At one year it will be 2 m tall and covered with flowers. It thickens a little thereafter but casts little shade and makes a sparse screen. Its life is short – about four years. Think of it as a rampant annual that gives a couple of bonus extra years. Casualties can be quickly replaced. *Sesbania* has so far been only tested in a warm climate with moderate to good rainfall.

**Keep a chemical-free garden** Before applying any chemicals, be sure that they will not harm the wildlife in your garden. Appreciate the creepy-crawlies for their beauty and adaptation to life, and the fact that many of them will have a beneficial effect in your garden. For example, some pollinate plants and others aerate the soil.

## Solanum giganteum

**Red bitter-apple**

**Size:** 2–3 x 2–3 m (wild), up to 2.5 x 2 m (garden)
**Natural habitat:** *Solanum* is found along a broad coastal strip from the southern Cape eastward, and then through much of the eastern interior. This shrub occurs in evergreen forest and in woodlands at middle altitudes, usually on sunny edges or in clearings.
**Growth form:** It is a small shrubby tree bearing weak spines. The leaves are large and bluish above, white below, quite striking but rather sparse. The brilliant red berries are borne in large heads from late summer onwards and greatly enjoyed by birds. The entire crop may be eaten in a single day when cold weather sets in.
**Propagation:** Seed.
**Uses:** This is not a conventional garden plant. It looks like an overgrown weed and indeed is a close kinsman to the dreaded alien bugweed – if slightly better looking. However, it is an asset in a bird garden, its berries often appearing in the first year. It is best placed among shrubs on the sunny edge of taller vegetation. *Solanum* grows at least 1.5 m in its first year, slowing down as it thickens. Mature plants die off after five to eight years. *Solanum* likes a temperate to warm summer with moderate to good rainfall.

## Sparrmannia africana

**Cape stock-rose**

**Size:** 3–5 x 4– m (wild), up to 3 x 4 m (garden)
**Natural habitat:** *Sparrmannia* is found naturally in the Eastern Cape, where it occurs on forest margins and among rocks.
**Growth form:** It is usually shrubby, branching down low even if single-stemmed. The foliage is dense, the leaves heart-shaped, huge and furry. *Sparrmannia* has lovely flowers: large and white with a central mass of yellow stamens. These appear in profusion in spring.
**Propagation:** Seed or cuttings.
**Uses:** *Sparrmannia* can be used as a specimen flowering shrub or for its foliage. It makes an adequate informal screen and is ideal for a new garden when instant results are needed. Flowering begins at two years and is reliable and showy thereafter. Growth is rapid – over 1 m per year, even in less than optimum conditions. Older plants continue to spread after full height is reached. *Sparrmannia* has a wide environmental tolerance, enjoying a warm or temperate summer with moderate to good rainfall. It survives a normal winter drought and moderate frost, although it loses its leaves in a cold winter. *Sparrmannia* grows well in a tub.

**Creating a garden colour scheme** Use a colour wheel when planning your shrubbery. You can create wonderful plant 'pictures' with contrasting and complementary colours. Nature's palette can be used to create a garden to suit your particular colour scheme.

## Strelitzia nicolai

### Wild banana

**Size:** 3–10 x 2–8 m (wild), up to 6 x 4 m (garden)
**Natural habitat:** This species is confined to the southeast coast. It is especially common in dune forest where its huge, waving leaves create tropical atmosphere.
**Growth form:** *S. nicolai* is solid and upright and always luxuriantly green. The banana bat *Pipistrellus nanus* roosts among the leaves. The flowers are bird-adapted. Large white sepals contrast with blue petals. The lower two petals are arranged so that a visiting bird is compelled to stand on them. Its weight parts them, exposing the pollen, which sticks to its breast. This cross-pollinates the next plant visited. The fruits are hard and woody, opening when mature, revealing black seeds covered with orange fluff. Despite a tough, unappetising texture, these attract barbets and starlings.
**Propagation:** Seed, or suckers taken from a parent plant.
**Uses:** *S. nicolai* makes a solo specimen in a tropical garden. It may not flower until seven years old but is reliable thereafter. It makes a lovely foliage plant in the interim. It is said that within the natural range, a grove of *S. nicolai* with its resident bats keeps mosquitoes away. It grows rapidly – at least 1 m per year. It can be grown inland provided that rainfall is at least moderate, and frost slight.

## Strelitzia reginae

### Crane flower

**Size:** 1.5 x 1.5 m (wild), up to 1.5 x 1.5 m (garden)
**Natural habitat:** *S. reginae* occurs in the Eastern Cape, where it grows in coastal scrub, and in parts of Zululand.
**Growth form:** It is always shrubby and rounded. It is a relative of the banana, with similar huge leaves. *S. reginae* flowers are striking and highly evolved to attract birds. The sepals are bright orange and vertical and serve as the advertising board. The petals are blue and the lower two are arranged so that a visiting bird is compelled to stand on them. Its weight causes them to part, exposing the pollen, which sticks to its breast. The bird automatically cross-pollinates the next plant visited. The fruit is a woody capsule, opening to reveal black seeds covered with orange fluff. Birds eat them.
**Propagation:** Seed, or suckers taken from a parent plant.
**Uses:** *S. reginae* is ideal for a small garden. It first flowers at four years, making a lovely foliage plant in the interim. Growth rate is about 30 cm per year. It likes a warm summer with good rainfall but survives well enough where the summer is temperate and rainfall moderate, provided that it is kept away from frost. Cut flowers last well and are sold world-wide.

**Rocks in the garden** Very few rocks are simply balanced on top of the soil. In nature they are nearly always partially buried, sometimes by as much as half their depth. Copy nature and you will get it right.

## Strophanthus petersianus

**Sand forest poison rope**

**Size:** 3–8 m long (wild), up to 5 m long (garden)
**Natural habitat:** This is a species of the eastern lowlands. It occurs in woodland and drier coastal forests.
**Growth form:** It is a slender creeper. The bark bears elaborate wings that assist climbing. The stunning sweetly scented flowers appear in spring. They are large open cups, produced in small clusters. The inside of the cup is cream, the outside pinkish. From the lip of the cup hang five twisted streamers, each 100 mm long. They are followed by bizarre fruits resembling a slender pair of ox-horns, each 30 cm long. These split to release seeds that have small fluffy parachutes, and blow away in the wind.
**Propagation:** Seed.
**Uses:** *S. petersianus* makes an ideal pergola or fence plant for a small garden. Trim the shoots back or twine them into the fence to keep control. Remember that creepers evolved to 'cheat' their way into the sun; although they manage in partial shade, flowers are produced at the top or on the sunny side of the plant, so site the plant accordingly. *S. petersianus* grows to full size within two to three years, thickening a little thereafter. It likes a warm climate with at least moderate rainfall.

## Strophanthus speciosus

**Poison rope**

**Size:** 3–10 x 2–5 m (wild), up to 3 x 4 m (garden)
**Natural habitat:** This species occurs in the Eastern Cape and the warmer parts of the east and north. It grows in evergreen forests and dense scrub, often in the deep shade.
**Growth form:** It is a scrambling shrub, capable of standing alone, but it will throw out long branches when support is available. The leaves are glossy and neatly veined. The flowers are outstanding, bright yellow with orange streaks at the base. The corolla lobes are long and thin and spirally twisted so that the flower looks like a spindly spider. Flowering is profuse in spring and lasts several months. The fruit resembles a small pair of ox-horns. When mature, it splits, releasing the seeds, which are carried away by the wind on little parachutes.
**Propagation:** Seed.
**Uses:** *S. speciosus* is one of the finest of all garden shrubs. The foliage is at all times brilliant, the flowers stunning. In full sun, flowering and fruiting commence at two years. If grown as a bush, *S. speciosus* forms a rounded mass. However, it is best grown against a fence or in a shrubbery where long, flowering branches can develop. It grows best in a warm temperate garden with good rainfall.

**Plants for a rockery** Choose plants carefully when creating a rockery. It takes a lot of trouble to get a rocky outcrop to look good, so select plants that won't cover the rocks within a season or two. Succulents look the part, without spreading too much.

## Syncolostemon densiflorus

**Pink plume**

**Size:** 1.5–2.5 x 1–2 m (wild), up to 2 x 1 m (garden)
**Natural habitat:** *Syncolostemon* is found naturally on the KwaZulu-Natal coast and Midlands, where it is found in grassland, on vlei margins and in low scrub alongside small streams.
**Growth form:** It is upright in form but always shrubby, branching low down even when single-stemmed. The foliage is undistinguished to look at but has a sweet herb-like smell when crushed. The flowers are beautiful pink tubes, produced in quantity almost throughout the year. Sunbirds are always in attendance.
**Propagation:** *Syncolostemon* cuttings take very easily, but seed has not been tried.
**Uses:** This is the perfect garden shrub, never getting too large, and can be cut back if it gets lanky. It makes a good flowering specimen and is best planted as a small thicket near the stoep to get the best value out of the birds. Flowering begins at two years. Growth rate is 1 m per year initially, maximum size being achieved within three years. *Syncolostemon* likes a temperate to warm summer with good rainfall. It dislikes drought.

## Syzygium pondoense

**Pondo waterwood**

**Size:** 1–3 x 1–2 m (wild), up to 2 x 1.5 m (garden)
**Natural habitat:** This is confined to sandstone soils in southern KwaZulu-Natal and the Eastern Cape. It fringes rocky rivers and is common alongside the Umtamvuna River.
**Growth form:** *S. pondoense* is a miniature tree. The trunk is white, contrasting with the rich purple of young twigs and leaf stalks. The leaves are outstanding, dark, glossy, narrow and all swept upwards. New red leaves are always present. The foliage exudes a pleasant myrtle-like scent when crushed. The flowers are conspicuous, white and pompon-like, consisting mainly of stamens. They are sweetly scented and attract all manner of insects, particularly brightly coloured beetles. Large, dark purple berries are produced in abundance, and these are relished by birds.
**Propagation:** Seed, which must be very fresh.
**Uses:** *S. pondoense* is one of the prettiest of all small shrubs. It grows about 40 cm per year. It flowers and fruits at two years, even outside its natural range. It also thrives in a range of garden conditions very different to those of its usual haunts, tolerating shale, high nutrient levels, heat, moderate drought and a little frost. However, *S. pondoense* grows best with a warm summer and high rainfall.

**Tubular flowers** Most red flowers are tubular, designed to favour birds, because they see red clearly, whereas many insects do not. The beaks of sunbirds are specially designed to probe these tubular red flowers, and sunbirds have become partially dependent on the flowers. This helps to guarantee pollination.

## Tarenna pavettoides

### False bride's bush

**Size:** 3–6 x 3–7 m (wild), up to 4 x 4 m (garden)
**Natural habitat:** *T. pavettoides* occurs from the Eastern Cape coast, through the warmer, wetter parts of KwaZulu-Natal to the eastern Escarpment. It grows primarily in swamp forest or alongside streams in coastal forest.
**Growth form:** It is usually shrubby but may be a single-stemmed tree. The leaves are large and pendulous, giving the plant a tropical look. Its flowers are small and white but produced in profusion and are sweetly scented. The fruits are small black berries, eaten by birds.
**Propagation:** Seed.
**Uses:** *T. pavettoides* is pretty enough to be used as a solo specimen. It can be used in a flowering screen or in a bird garden and is ideal for a soggy hollow where nothing much else will grow. It looks its best beside water. First flowers appear at three years and fruit is produced outside the natural range. Growth is rapid – at least 80 cm per year. *T. pavettoides* must have high rainfall or a damp position, growing equally well in or out of the shade. It likes a warm summer and cannot tolerate frost.

## Tarenna supra-axillaris

### Narrow-leaved false bride's bush

**Size:** 2–5 x 2–5 m (wild), up to 3 x 3 m (garden)
**Natural habitat:** This species is found naturally in Zululand and the warmer parts of the northeast. It occurs in sand forest, in fire-proof spots in sandy grassland and in thickets alongside rocky streams.
**Growth form:** It is nearly always shrubby but upright. *T. supra-axillaris* invariably looks freshly groomed. The white twigs are all neatly upswept, the effect being complemented by the vertically borne, glossy, narrow leaves. Its flowers are small and white but produced in profusion and are sweetly scented. The fruits are small black berries, eaten by birds.
**Propagation:** Seed.
**Uses:** *T. supra-axillaris* makes a lovely small specimen, the foliage always looking good. It is ideal for a small garden. First flowers appear at three years and fruit is produced outside the natural range. Growth rate is about 40 cm per year, so it grows a bit too slowly to make a good screen. *T. supra-axillaris* must have a warm summer with moderate to good rainfall. It is moderately drought-hardy and withstands a little frost.

**White bounty** Many indigenous plants bear white flowers. The white colour of the petals is due to the absence of pigment; the intensity of whiteness is caused by air spaces that reflect light.

## Tecomaria capensis

**Cape honeysuckle**

**Size:** 3–4 x 4–7 m (wild), up to 3 x 5 m (garden)
**Natural habitat:** *Tecomaria* occurs from the southern Cape through much of KwaZulu-Natal to the eastern Lowveld. It is found in dense, deciduous woodland and on forest margins.
**Growth form:** It is a vigorous shrub that tends to sprawl as it gets older. *Tecomaria* is famous for its flowers. These are tubular and asymmetrical, one tip elongating and curving over to form a hood. The natural colour varies from mid- to dark orange; yellow seems confined to horticulture. Flowering is profuse throughout much of spring and summer and even in winter a few flowers are often present. Sunbirds like the flowers.
**Propagation:** Cuttings.
**Uses:** Because it is untidy, this shrub does not make a good specimen. Moreover, long branches that touch the ground form roots, producing an expanding colony best placed in a shrubbery or on a boundary. Yellow-flowering forms are notably smaller and more compact. However, sunbirds prefer natural colours. Older plants flower best when cut back every year or two. Growth is rapid, at least 1 m per year, and flowering begins in the second year. *Tecomaria* prefers a warm climate but grows reasonably well in a temperate summer. It is winter-deciduous under marginal conditions.

## Tephrosia pondoensis

**Pondo poison pea**

**Size:** 3–5 x 2–4 m (wild), up to 4 x 3 m (garden)
**Natural habitat:** This species of shrub is one of a very diverse community restricted to coarse sandy soils peculiar to Pondoland sandstone in southern KwaZulu-Natal and the Eastern Cape. It occurs on forest edges and is common alongside the Umtamvuna River.
**Growth form:** *Tephrosia* is a rounded but erect shrub. The leaves are divided into tiny delicate leaflets and droop gracefully. The flowers are pea-shaped and borne in small bunches on branch tips. The colour is luminous pale orange, framed with darker orange, and most attractive. The fruit is a small pod that splits to release its seeds.
**Propagation:** Seed.
**Uses:** *Tephrosia* is a most decorative shrub, worth a prime spot. It also makes a good screen. Speed of growth is rewarding – at least 1 m per year, and flowering begins in the second year. Plants grown in semi-shade have paler flowers. Despite a restricted natural distribution where the climate is warm and rainfall good, *Tephrosia* grows well in drier places and tolerates some frost. It is not dependent upon nutrient-poor, sandy soil, growing in most soils in cultivation.

**Covering large areas** Stabilising a steep bank with sprawling shrubs is practical and attractive. Use *Tecomaria capensis* mixed with blue *Plumbago auriculata*; *Bauhinia galpinii* provides a tough and spreading cover for very large areas.

## Tetradenia riparia

### Misty plume bush

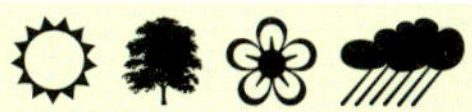

**Size:** 2–3 x 2–3 m (wild), up to 2 x 2 m (garden)
**Natural habitat:** *Tetradenia* is found naturally in the warm, wetter parts of the east. It usually fringes small watercourses or forest margins.
**Growth form:** It is a fairly sparse, softly woody shrub. The leaves are large and furry and the whole plant has a soft texture. The flowers are pale mauve and although small, are produced in huge branching masses that seem to outweigh the rest of the plant. Flowering is most prolific during winter but continues at lesser pace almost throughout the year.
**Propagation:** Cuttings.
**Uses:** Once established *Tetradenia* soon generates a little colony. Note that only the male plants produce the marvellous flowering displays; females are comparatively dowdy. Growth is rapid – about 80 cm per year – and flowering takes place in the first year. This is not an ideal hedge plant, being too flimsy, and it rarely makes a complete screen. It is best used beside a water feature or on the edge of a forest clump. If *Tetradenia* gets too straggly, it responds well to vigorous pruning. This shrub likes moderate to high rainfall and a temperate to warm summer. It languishes in drought and tolerates only the slightest frost.

## Thunbergia alata

### Black-eyed Susan

**Size:** 3–5 m long (wild), up to 4 m long (garden)
**Natural habitat:** It ranges from the Eastern Cape through the warmer, wetter areas eastwards and northwards. It is common on forest edges but more often seen in human-modified areas along roadsides.
**Growth form:** It is a soft, twining creeper, flowering almost throughout the year, with a summer peak. Usually the flowers are flaring bright orange trumpets with a deep maroon throat. Sometimes they are yellow, and a near-white form exists. In colder areas *Thunbergia* gets cut back by frost, and growth begins again in spring. Birds like nesting in the dense foliage.
**Propagation:** Seed, and cuttings that root relatively easily in sand during summer.
**Uses:** This is the perfect creeper for most gardens. It grows quickly, without getting rampant. It needs support such as a fence and is ideal for a screening trellis. It is too small for most pergolas. *Thunbergia* grows to full size within a single season, with the first flowers appearing within days of planting. Most colour forms are available commercially, the rarer colours being favoured by nurseries. *Thunbergia* flowers better if cut back a bit in early spring. It seeds readily in gardens, so replacements are always ready. It likes high rainfall.

**Creating variety** If you want to break the monotony of a large expanse of lawn, plant one or more interesting groups of shrubs. Single shrubs dotted about your lawn tend to make it look smaller.

## Tinnea barbata

**Purple tinnea**

**Size:** 1–2 x 1–2 m (wild), up to 1.5 x 1.5 m (garden)
**Natural habitat:** *Tinnea* is indigenous to Mpumalanga where it occurs in riverine vegetation, sometimes in the shade.
**Growth form:** This species is always shrubby and soft-textured. The leaves are small and furry, and the shrub is evergreen. The flowers are its greatest charm. These are mauve or violet rather than purple, and asymmetric, the lowest petal being much larger than the other four. The fruits are little hollow hanging balloons.
**Propagation:** Cuttings.
**Uses:** *Tinnea* makes a wonderful garden plant. Cuttings flower within a year of striking. Subsequently, *Tinnea* is never without flowers and puts on a fine show for about five months in spring and summer. Although performing well enough in partial shade, *Tinnea* flowers much better in full sunshine. It likes a warm climate with moderate to good rainfall, although it tolerates short, dry spells. It is frost-sensitive but small enough to protect on the sunny north-facing side of a wall or shrubbery. A related species, *T. rhodesiana*, occurs in the far northeast. It has deep maroon flowers but is otherwise virtually identical to *T. barbata*. Its performance is similar, except that it prefers partial shade and good rainfall.

## Tricalysia capensis

**Cape coffee**

**Size:** 2–5 x 2–5 m (wild), up to 3 x 3 m (garden)
**Natural habitat:** This species ranges from the Eastern Cape, through KwaZulu-Natal to the far northeast, avoiding the colder uplands. It occurs in the undergrowth of forests or at their edges, or on isolated rock outcrops in wetter areas.
**Growth form:** *T. capensis* is always multi-stemmed but neat and erect, with lovely glossy foliage. It is noted for its displays of sweetly scented white flowers that may cover the plant. These are followed by red berries, sometimes turning black, clustered at the base of each leaf. These are also attractive, although apparently not very popular with birds.
**Propagation:** Seed.
**Uses:** *T. capensis* is an ideal specimen shrub, both for foliage and flowers. Flowering begins at three years but is not as exuberant in semi-shade as it is in full sun. Fruiting has not so far been seen outside the natural range. Growth rate is about 40 cm per year – a bit slow to make a good screen. *T. capensis* enjoys a warm summer with moderate to good rainfall but withstands an average winter drought. Unlike the other species of *Tricalysia*, *T. capensis* tolerates some frost. It is small enough to be sheltered if planted in the correct spot.

**Scale your planting** If you have a small garden, pay careful consideration to the scale of your planting. Use small trees and dainty shrubs, such as *Tinnea* or *Myrsine*, and remember to leave some open spaces. These add scale, and enable everything to be seen.

## Tricalysia lanceolata

### Common tricalysia

**Size:** 3–7 x 3–7 m (wild), up to 4 x 4 m (garden)
**Natural habitat:** This species ranges from the Eastern Cape, through the warmer parts of Kwazulu-Natal to the far north-east. It is most common in the undergrowth of evergreen forest, although it may be found in almost any wooded habitat.
**Growth form:** It tends to be an upright shrub. The bark has perfectly regular pin-stripe furrows. The leaves are glossy dark green and most attractive. *T. lanceolata* is noted for its profuse displays of sweetly scented white flowers. Flowering takes place in early spring and makes a fine show even in partial shade. Flowers are followed by attractive red berries that mature to black and are eaten by birds.
**Propagation:** Seed.
**Uses:** This is one of the most attractive of all larger shrubs and is especially useful because it performs well in light shade. Flowering begins at three years, making *T. lanceolata* an ideal specimen. Growth is reasonably fast – at least 50 cm per year. This shrub enjoys a warm summer with moderate to good rainfall, but withstands an average winter drought. *T. lanceolata* tolerates a little frost.

## Tricalysia sonderiana

### Dune tricalysia

**Size:** 3–7 x 3–7 m (wild), up to 5 x 5 m (garden)
**Natural habitat:** This species is found naturally on the KwaZulu-Natal coast. It occurs on the edges of evergreen forests and is common in dune forest.
**Growth form:** It is always erect, even if shrubby. The bark of older plants has a nice furrowed pattern. The leaves are dark and leathery and *T. sonderiana* is densely evergreen. It is noted for its sweetly scented white flowers, which make a wonderful display in spring. They are little narrow white bells with fluffy throats, which hang shoulder-to-shoulder along every branchlet. These are followed by red berries that mature to black. The berries are also attractive and are eaten by birds.
**Propagation:** Seed.
**Uses:** *T. sonderiana* is an ideal foliage and flowering shrub. It is especially useful in beach gardens. Flowering begins at three years. Fruiting has so far been noted only within the natural range. Growth rate is about 40 cm per year, a bit slow to make a good wind-break. *T. sonderiana* enjoys a warm summer with moderate to good rainfall but withstands an average winter drought. Frost-hardiness is slight.

**The natural look** Try to create natural-looking rocky outcrops when using rocks in your garden – you don't want to end up with an ugly, artificial-looking conglomeration of rocks and stones. The rocks need to look as if they ended up there naturally.

## Trichocladus crinitus

**Onderbos, Black witch-hazel**

**Size:** 2–4 x 2–4 m (wild), up to 2.5 x 2 m (garden)
**Natural habitat:** *T. crinitus* is a coastal species that occurs from Knysna to Zululand. It grows in the undergrowth of evergreen forests and dominates in parts of the Knysna Forest.
**Growth form:** It is often shrubby. The foliage is exceptionally attractive. The leaves are glossy dark green above, with a very pale green undersurface embellished with ginger hairs on the larger veins. The flowers are distinctive, with narrow petals massing into ragged spherical heads. Flower petals are yellow and spidery and each flowering head has a deep red centre. Flowering takes place in late winter.
**Propagation:** Seed or cuttings.
**Uses:** *T. crinitus* is a particularly attractive shrub, worth growing for both foliage and flowers, and is especially useful because it looks its best in half-shade. It is the ideal filler for a forest clump. Flowering begins at about five years. Growth rate is about 40 cm per year. *T. crinitus* demands high rainfall but grows equally well in a warm or temperate summer. It is sensitive to drought and frost and in warmer areas it dislikes full sunshine.

## Trichocladus ellipticus

**White witch-hazel**

**Size:** 3–6 x 3–5 m (wild), up to 3 x 3 m (garden)
**Natural habitat:** This species occurs in coastal and mist-belt forests from the southern Cape, through KwaZulu-Natal to the far northeast of the country.
**Growth form:** It may be shrubby or single-stemmed but is always erect. The foliage is exceptionally attractive and gives a new dimension to the term bi-coloured; the leaf is dark glossy green, the undersurface being a rich, textured pale ginger. Every vein appears to be highlighted. Young growth is covered with a golden fur. The flowers are small and white, sweet smelling, and borne in tiny bunches. Flowering takes place in summer.
**Propagation:** Seed or cuttings.
**Uses:** *T. ellipticus* is a particularly attractive shrub, one of the finest foliage plants of all. It is especially useful because it looks its best in half-shade. In cooler areas it also grows well enough in full sun. It grows about 40 cm per year. Flowering begins at about five years. *T. ellipticus* demands high rainfall but grows equally well in a warm or temperate summer. It is sensitive to drought and frost.

**Curves are better** Use a sun-warmed hosepipe to mark out gentle curves for garden beds and shrubbery boundaries. A few generous curves are better than a series of little ripples.

## Turraea obtusifolia

**Small honeysuckle tree**

**Size:** 1–3 x 1–3 m (wild), up to 1.5 x 1.5 m (garden)
**Natural habitat:** *Turraea* ranges from the Eastern Cape through the warmer, wetter parts of KwaZulu-Natal to the far northeast. It is most common in sparse rocky woodlands but is also found in dune forest.
**Growth form:** It is an erect dainty shrub. The leaves are small, neat and glossy and arranged in tidy bunches. The flowers are snow-white and may cover the plant in midsummer. The fruit is green, even when mature, and has the general look of a small, segmented, peeled orange. On a dry day, when the fruit is ripe, it splits along the segment boundaries and the outer casing peels back, revealing a tightly packed mass of orange seeds, so only fully ripe seed is offered to the eager birds.
**Propagation:** Seed.
**Uses:** *Turraea* makes a delightful garden plant. It can be grown as a specimen in the smallest garden or could be massed on the sunny edge of a shrubbery. It is worth growing for the flowering display and for its bird-attracting powers. It is slow-growing, typically about 40 cm per year, but it first flowers at three years, and profusely thereafter. It likes a warm summer, with at least moderate rainfall.

## Uvaria caffra

**Small cluster-pear**

**Size:** 1–3 x 1–2 m (wild), up to 2 x 1 m (garden)
**Natural habitat:** *Uvaria* is indigenous to the Eastern Cape and KwaZulu-Natal coast, extending inland in northern Zululand. It occurs most frequently in evergreen forests and may dominate the undergrowth.
**Growth form:** It is a small shrub with a tendency to scramble. The foliage is very attractive, the leaves being clean-cut and glossy, especially the undersurface. The fruit is very distinctive, with a passing resemblance to a little hand with stubby fingers. It has about six fingers and is yellow and waxy. *Uvaria* is the host plant of *Graphium* butterflies.
**Propagation:** Seed.
**Uses:** *Uvaria* makes a delightful foliage plant and is a good addition to a wildlife garden. It is best grown against a support but will stand alone if scrambling shoots are threaded back into the rest of the foliage. Fruits first appear at four years within the natural range but have yet to be seen outside it. Rate of growth is about 40 cm per year, except for a few long fronds sprouting occasionally. *Uvaria* grows best in partial shade. It likes a warm summer with moderate to good rainfall. It is probably frost-sensitive but easily protected by proper siting.

**Ideal trellis creepers** Trellises need relatively delicate creepers that will not get out of hand. *Cnestis, Monanthotaxis* and *Uvaria* are all excellent for this purpose.

# INDEX

# GLOSSARY

**Asymmetrical:** not symmetric; unevenly divided

**Cell sap:** fluid in the plant cells

**Compound leaf:** a leaf divided into separate leaflets

**Dominant:** most common species in a habitat, sometimes outnumbering all others combined

**Endemic:** found only in a particular area

**Epiphytic:** rooted in leaf litter in tree forks: not parasitic

**Locally common:** common in some parts of their natural range

**Multi-stemmed:** having a trunk dividing at or below ground level

**Mulch:** a permeable material such as compost, dead leaves, humus, well rotted manure or small stones used to cover the soil to reduce evaporation

**Natural range:** the geographical area in which a species grows naturally

**Petiole:** a leaf stalk

**Riverine thicket:** dense vegetation lining river banks

**Scramble:** lean, sprawl or otherwise grow over surrounding vegetation

**Single-species stand:** a plant community consisting of just one species

**Specimen:** a plant of a species with an elegant profile, good looking enough to be planted as an individual feature

**Stamen:** pollen-producing part of a flower

**Stand:** grove, small community

**Style:** a female component of a flower

## SYMBOLS

 Grows best in full sun

 Grows best in partial shade

 Grows best in shade

 Deciduous shrub (loses its leaves)

 Evergreen shrub (never loses its leaves)

 Scrambler (no thick trunk, grows over surrounding vegetation)

 Flowers are an attractive feature

 Fruit is an attractive feature

 Attracts butterflies

 Attracts birds

 Attracts bats

 Grows well in clay

 Survives severe drought

 Survives moderate drought

 Grows well in coastal sand and withstands coastal wind

 Grows in waterlogged soil

 Survives harsh frost

 Survives moderate frost

 Survives light frost

**No frost symbol:** Cannot survive frost

 Grows best in area with high rainfall

 Grows best in area with moderate rainfall

 Grows best in area with low rainfall